PREFACE

1. Scope

This publication provides doctrine for planning and executing operations to protect a joint security area in operational areas outside the homeland. It outlines the joint force commander's (JFC's) responsibilities and discusses organizational options, and command and control considerations across the range of military operations. It focuses on joint security operations that are designed to protect bases and lines of communications that support joint operations.

2. Purpose

This publication has been prepared under the direction of the Chairman of the Joint Chiefs of Staff. It sets forth joint doctrine to govern the activities and performance of the Armed Forces of the United States in joint operations and provides the doctrinal basis for interagency coordination and for US military involvement in multinational operations. It provides military guidance for the exercise of authority by combatant commanders and other JFCs and prescribes joint doctrine for operations, education, and training. It provides military guidance for use by the Armed Forces in preparing their appropriate plans. It is not the intent of this publication to restrict the authority of the JFC from organizing the force and executing the mission in a manner the JFC deems most appropriate to ensure unity of effort in the accomplishment of the overall objective.

3. Application

a. Joint doctrine established in this publication applies to the Joint Staff, commanders of combatant commands, subunified commands, joint task forces, subordinate components of these commands, and the Services.

b. The guidance in this publication is authoritative; as such, this doctrine will be followed except when, in the judgment of the commander, exceptional circumstances dictate otherwise. If conflicts arise between the contents of this publication and the contents of Service publications, this publication will take precedence unless the Chairman of the Joint Chiefs of Staff, normally in coordination with the other members of the Joint Chiefs of Staff, has provided more current and specific guidance. Commanders of forces operating as part of a multinational (alliance or coalition) military command should follow multinational doctrine and procedures ratified by the United States. For doctrine and procedures not ratified by the United States, commanders should evaluate and follow the multinational command's doctrine and procedures, where applicable and consistent with US law, regulations, and doctrine.

For the Chairman of the Joint Chiefs of Staff:

LLOYD J. AUSTIN III
Lieutenant General, USA
Director, Joint Staff

SUMMARY OF CHANGES
REVISION OF JOINT PUBLICATION 3-10
DATED 01 AUGUST 2006

- The role of land forces in joint security operations was expanded to include the utilization of the US Army's maneuver enhancement brigades.

- The discussion of the joint force maritime component commander's role in joint security operations was expanded.

- Naval expeditionary support force and naval expeditionary support force commander terms were changed to maritime expeditionary security force and maritime expeditionary security force commander respectively.

- The language on the naval expeditionary logistics support group was expanded.

- Chemical, biological, radiological, nuclear, and high-yield explosive language was replaced to reflect extant chemical, biological, radiological, and nuclear language.

- The term battlespace was replaced with operational environment where applicable.

- Language on the utility of nonlethal weapons for joint security operations was added.

- Mobility corridor was changed to movement corridor consistent with current usage.

- The following terms and definitions were recommended for deletion from Joint Publication 1-02: Army base; axial route; base defense zone; combat support elements; combat support troops; high-water mark; joint line of communications security board; naval coastal warfare; naval coastal warfare commander; perimeter defense; and rear area; and rear guard.

- Publication references were updated.

- Redundancies were removed and proper references provided.

Intentionally Blank

TABLE OF CONTENTS

CHAPTER V
LINES OF COMMUNICATIONS SECURITY

APPENDIX

GLOSSARY

FIGURE

- **Provides an Overview of Joint Security Environment**

- **Describes Command and Control of Joint Security Forces**

- **Discusses Joint Security Operations Planning**

- **Covers Base and Base Cluster Security Operations**

- **Describes Lines of Communications Security**

Overview

Our National Security Strategy, National Defense Strategy, and National Military Strategy call for deployed military units, forward-based activities, and forward operating bases.

The security environment requires that deployed military units, forward-based activities, and forward operating bases protect themselves against threats designed to interrupt, interfere, or impair the effectiveness of joint operations. **Base and lines of communications (LOCs) security** must be properly planned, prepared, executed, and assessed to prevent or mitigate hostile actions against US personnel, resources, facilities, equipment, and information.

Joint security areas (JSAs) are increasingly vulnerable to enemy forces with sophisticated surveillance devices, accurate weapon systems, and transport assets capable of inserting forces behind friendly combat formations.

Levels of Threat

Threat activities can be generally described and categorized in three levels. Each level or any combination of levels may exist in the operational area, independently or simultaneously.

Typical **Level I threats** include enemy agents and terrorists whose primary missions include espionage, sabotage, and subversion. Enemy activity and individual terrorist attacks may include random or directed killing of military and civilian personnel, kidnapping, and/or guiding special-purpose individuals or teams to targets.

Level II threats include small-scale, irregular forces conducting unconventional warfare that can pose serious threats to military forces and civilians. These attacks can cause significant disruptions to military operations as well as the orderly conduct of local government and services.

Level III threats may be encountered when a threat force has the capability of projecting combat power by air, land, or sea, anywhere into the operational area. Level III threats necessitate a decision to commit a tactical combat force (TCF) or other significant available forces to counter the threat. This threat level is beyond the capability of base and base cluster defense and response forces.

A JSA is a specific surface area designated to facilitate protection of bases. The size of a JSA may vary considerably and is highly dependent on the size of the operational area, mission essential assets, logistic support requirements, threat, or scope of the joint operation.

Base functions include force projection, movement control, sustainment, command and control. Base nodes are air bases, airfields, seaports, and sea bases.

Command and Control

Unity of command is fundamental to effective security within the joint security area.

To provide security and unity of command the joint force commander (JFC) designates operational areas, selects appropriate command structures, and establishes a command and control network through multinational, subordinate, and adjacent commanders to direct and coordinate the actions of components and supporting organizations or agencies.

The chief of mission (COM) is responsible for the direction, coordination, and supervision of all US Government executive branch employees in that country (except those under the command of a US area military commander). Geographic combatant commander (GCC) and COM security memorandums of agreement (MOAs) do not alter established command relationships, nor relieve commanders of responsibility for unit security. The GCC has responsibility for all Department of Defense (DOD) elements and personnel within that geographic area of responsibility (AOR), except those for whom security responsibility has been transferred to the COM via the MOA process.

A GCC is ultimately responsible for all military joint security operations (JSO) conducted in the AOR. GCCs establish AOR-wide force protection measures, procedures, and policies for joint forces, family members, DOD civilian workforce, and designated government contractor employees that are assigned, attached, in-transit, or otherwise physically located within their AORs. The functional combatant commander coordinates with the applicable GCC and/or subordinate JFC to ensure that these facilities or bases are adequately secured. Subordinate JFCs have the authority to organize forces to best accomplish the assigned mission based on their concept of operations and provide security of all military bases and LOCs within their joint operations area. The JFC dedicates assets for JSO in proportion to the severity of the threat in order to conserve resources and prevent degradation of support.

The JFC, normally through a designated joint security coordinator, ensures that appropriate command relationships among subordinate areas, base, and base cluster commanders are established and understood by all affected commands. Tactical control is the typical command relationship established between the base or base cluster commander and the dedicated security force, when the attached force is from a different component command.

Commanders may plan, coordinate, monitor, advise, and direct JSOs through joint security coordination centers, rear area operations centers, rear tactical operations centers, base cluster operations centers, and base defense operations centers.

Joint Security Operation Planning

Understanding the basic fundamentals of joint security operations is key to the proper execution of this challenging mission.

The fundamentals of JSO planning are as follows:

- Establish clear joint security related command and control relationships and responsibilities.

- Understand the enemy.

- See the operational environment.

- Use the defenders' advantages.

- Mitigate defenders' disadvantages.

- Balance security actions with civil and political considerations.

Base and LOC security should be governed by the factors of mission, enemy, terrain and weather, troops and support available — time available (METT-T).

Mission

The primary mission of the base is to support joint force objectives. Inherent in this mission is the subsidiary mission of securing these bases and LOCs from enemy action.

Enemy

Every intelligence and counterintelligence resource available to the base commander should be used to determine enemy capabilities and intentions.

Terrain and Weather

The base commander must make **the best use of the terrain** within the operational area. Commanders analyzing terrain must consider all its military aspects, from the standpoints of base and LOC function as well as security considerations from both a defender's and enemy's perspective.

Weather and visibility conditions can have a significant impact on land, air, and maritime operations. Commanders should minimize their own vulnerabilities to adverse weather conditions and exploit any advantages over enemy vulnerabilities.

Troops and Support Available

There may be some units on a base whose primary missions are defense and security. In some cases, the JFC or subordinate commander may determine that land combat forces, usually platoon to battalion task force level, may also be assigned as dedicated base, surface LOC and/or area defense forces. In other cases, particularly bases where there are limited combat forces, security forces may be formed from logistic, transiting units, or other support units.

Time Available

Commanders assess the time available for planning, preparing, and executing the mission. They consider how friendly or adversary forces will use the time and the possible results. Proper use of the time available can fundamentally alter the situation. Time available is normally defined in terms of the missions and tasks assigned and bounded by adversary capabilities.

Planning Considerations

In planning for JSO, the following are common considerations.

- Force protection.

- Intelligence.

- Communications.

- Chemical, biological, radiological, and nuclear defense.

- Air and missile defense.

- Threat early warning and alert notification system.

- Land forces and joint security.

- Maritime-land interface.

- Terrain management and infrastructure development.

- Area damage control.

- Integration of joint security and logistic operations.

- Detainee operations.

Other major planning considerations are host-nation support; multinational operations; civil-military operations; interagency, intergovernmental organization, and nongovernmental organization coordination; DOD civilian work force and DOD contractor employees; and laws, agreements, and other legal constraints.

Base and Base Cluster Security Operations

The joint force commander assigns and controls forces that are responsible to execute base and base cluster security operations.

Key to establishing successful base security is to ensure there is a proactive base security posture. Security forces must be trained, organized, and equipped to properly execute base and base cluster security against Level I and II threats, and if required, be prepared to engage Level III threats.

In Level I and II environments, actions against enemy threats and other potential emergencies to include natural disasters and accidents must be planned for and adjustments to base or base cluster security plans made. Base security forces should have a **high degree of direct-fire lethality** to cope with potential threats. The mobile security force (MSF) should also have access to supporting indirect fires, a high degree of tactical mobility and a reasonable span of command and control. The MSF commander must have the most up-to-date copy of the base defense plan, and, when applicable, base cluster defense plan in order to effectively coordinate between the base and MSF operations. Control measures in base and base cluster security operations are the same as those used in defensive operations. The area commanders/base cluster commanders coordinate **base boundaries**, establish phase lines, contact points, objectives, and checkpoints as necessary to control the base clusters. The **base boundary** is not necessarily the base perimeter, rather it should be established based upon the factors of METT-T, specifically balancing the need of the base defense forces to control key terrain with their ability to accomplish the mission. These measures decrease the likelihood of fratricide, prevent noncombatant casualties, and minimize damage to the property of friendly civilians. Perimeter primary positions must be prepared to prevent hostile forces from penetrating the base and interfering with its primary mission. **If not capable of defeating enemy threats, the security forces must delay the enemy until the MSF can respond.** Other base security considerations are: direct fire weapon systems; antiarmor weapons; indirect fire systems; close air and other aviation support; coastal and harbor security support; vulnerability to release of toxic industrial materials; barriers, obstacles and mines; physical facilities; as well as operations security and deception in support of operations security.

In some operations, there may be a Level III threat. In these situations, the JFC must consider and plan for combat operations in the JSA. Area commanders assigned a JSA as part of their area of operations must develop and organize TCFs and/or port security units that are trained, led, and equipped to concentrate the necessary combat power at the decisive time and place. Defeating Level III threats within the JSA will ensure support bases can continue vital sustainment operations.

Level III threats can result from enemy forces infiltrating or penetrating friendly positions and moving into the friendly operational area, or conducting airborne, air assault, or amphibious operations. The designated land force commander has several options to deal with the threat. The commander may establish a TCF to deal with such a threat; designate another force as the on-order TCF; or, accept the risk of not having a designated TCF. If required, the commander may establish a number of TCFs, in accordance with the Level III threat and the JFC's guidance.

Lines of Communications Security

Secure lines of communications (LOCs) are vital to successful joint operations.

In some operational environments, **the greatest risk to joint force operations may be the threat to the main supply routes** from the ports of debarkation forward to the main battle area or forward operating bases.

Fundamentals of LOC security.

Fundamentally, **three tenets are noteworthy with regard to LOC security**. First, LOC security is an operation, not a logistic function; secondly, LOC security against Level II and Level III threats will require dedicated security force capabilities; and third, LOC actions and operations must be closely synchronized with joint movement control operations.

The primary threats to movement along ground LOCs in Level I and II threat environments are mines, ambushes, improvised explosive devices and vehicle-borne improvised explosive devices. Improvised explosive devices and vehicle-borne improvised explosive devices may incorporate chemical or radiological material to create exposure and contamination hazards. Level III threats may include risk from air and ground conventional force interdiction. Land LOCs, rail lines and pipelines may also be vulnerable to demolitions, sniper fire, and indirect fire. Both active and passive security measures, to include reconnaissance and surveillance, should be employed.

Active measures include cordon security operations that support a specific route for a designated period during which multiple movements take place. Passive measures include capitalizing on security offered by other activities not directly related to LOC security.

Reconnaissance and surveillance should include the terrain along the LOCs that the enemy could use to influence the joint force's movement and should take place at irregular intervals to avoid developing a regular pattern that an enemy force could exploit.

CONCLUSION

This publication provides doctrine for planning and executing operations to protect a JSA outside the homeland. It outlines the JFC's responsibilities and discusses organizational options, and command and control considerations across the range of military operations. It focuses on JSO that are designed to protect bases and LOCs that support joint operations.

CHAPTER I
OVERVIEW

> *"The protection function encompasses a number of tasks, including . . . securing and protecting JSAs [joint security areas]."*
>
> **Joint Publication 3-0,** *Joint Operations*

1. Introduction

a. Our National Security Strategy, National Defense Strategy, and National Military Strategy call for deployed military units, forward-based activities, and forward operating bases. The security environment requires that these units, activities, and bases protect themselves against threats designed to interrupt, interfere, or impair the effectiveness of joint operations. Base and lines of communications (LOCs) security must be properly planned, prepared, executed, and assessed to prevent or mitigate hostile actions against US personnel, resources, facilities, equipment, and information.

b. This publication provides **guidelines for planning, preparing for, executing and assessing operations to protect a joint security area (JSA) outside the homeland.** Within this publication, these operations will be referred to as joint security operations (JSO). JSO provide for the defense of and facilitate force protection (FP) actions for designated bases, base clusters, LOCs, and other designated areas. They provide for unity of effort and efficient use of constrained resources to maintain a relatively secure environment allowing the joint force commander (JFC) and component commanders to focus on their primary mission. JSO may entail the participation of host nation (HN) forces, to include various police or security forces (SF). The JFC should establish the operational framework that best addresses the operational environment while providing for maximum flexibility. **The designation of a JSA is normally based on the nature of the threat, type and scope of the mission, and the size of the operational area.**

c. This publication also outlines joint security coordinator (JSC) responsibilities and discusses joint security organizational options and command and control (C2) considerations.

2. Joint Security Environment

a. A geographic combatant commander (GCC) or a subordinate JFC must be prepared to protect bases, base clusters, airfields, seaports, sustainment activities and LOCs within the operational area. JSAs are increasingly vulnerable to enemy forces with sophisticated surveillance devices, accurate weapon systems, and transport assets capable of inserting forces behind friendly combat formations. In noncontiguous situations, these forces may operate within the operational areas of friendly forces. **Standoff weapon threats in the form of improvised explosive devices (IEDs), mortars, rockets, theater missiles, and surface-to-air missiles (SAMs) are of particular concern.**

b. JSAs may be small or may span national boundaries, each with a distinct security environment and different policies and resources to address threats. They will normally contain units, surface LOCs, and facilities from all elements of the joint force, supporting commands, organizations, intergovernmental agencies, nongovernmental organizations (NGOs), as well as important HN infrastructure. It will often contain the units and facilities of one or more multinational partners. Most of these units and facilities are organized into bases and base clusters to enhance their effectiveness and security. Vital sea and air LOCs, through which the bulk of logistic support flows, have their greatest vulnerability where they converge, often times at the aerial ports of debarkation (APODs) or seaports of debarkation (SPODs).

c. **Levels of Threat. There are three levels of threat as depicted in Figure I-1.** These different levels provide a general description and categorization of threat activities, identify recommended security responses to counter them, and establish a common reference for planning. Each level or any combination of levels may exist in the operational area independently or simultaneously. Emphasis on specific base or LOC security measures may depend on the anticipated level of threat. This does not imply that threat activities will occur in a specific sequence or that there is a necessary interrelationship between each level.

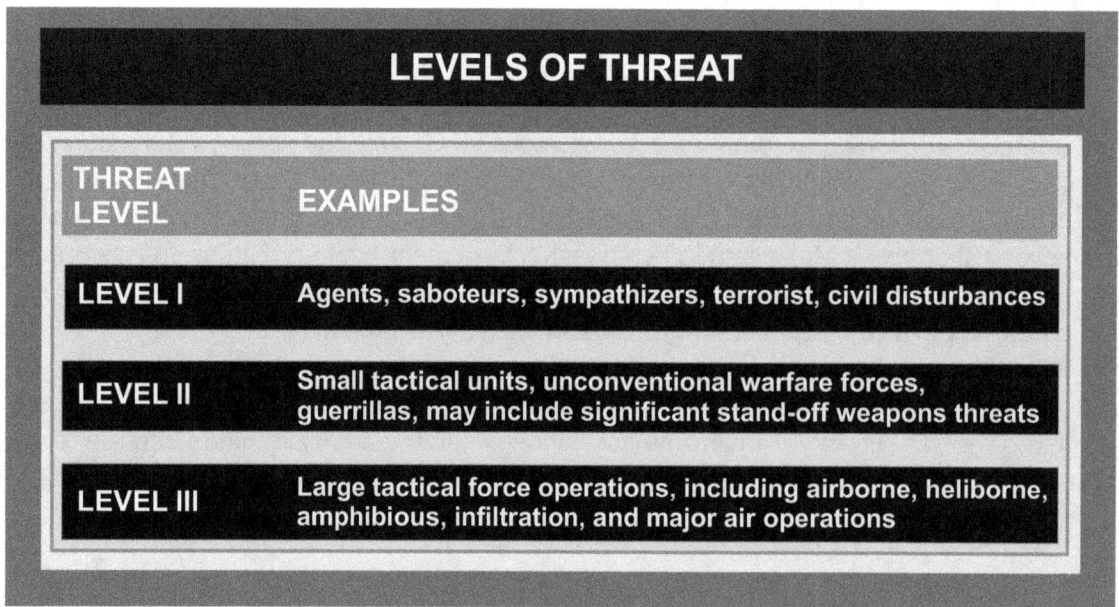

Figure I-1. Levels of Threat

d. Commanders and JSCs must be aware that chemical, biological, radiological, and nuclear (CBRN) materials may be used at any level of threat. CBRN materials may be used by terrorists or unconventional forces in order to accomplish their political or military objectives, or in conjunction with air, missile or other conventional force attacks.

For additional information on CBRN defensive considerations see Joint Publication (JP) 3-11, Operations in Chemical, Biological, Radiological, and Nuclear (CBRN) Environments.

e. While the doctrinal principles and guidelines provided herein are applicable to all threats, their **primary focus is on Level I and II threats.**

(1) **Level I Threats.** Typical Level I threats include enemy agents and terrorists whose primary missions include espionage, sabotage, and subversion. Enemy activity and individual terrorist attacks may include random or directed killing of military and civilian personnel, kidnapping, and/or guiding special-purpose individuals or teams to targets. Level I threat tactics may also include hijacking air, land, and sea vehicles for use in direct attacks; the use of IEDs, random sniping, vehicle-borne improvised explosive devices (VBIEDs), SAMs, and/or individual grenade and rocket propelled grenade attacks. Civilians sympathetic to the enemy may become significant threats to US and multinational operations. They may be the most difficult to counter because they are normally not part of an established enemy agent network and their actions may be random and unpredictable. Countering criminal activities and civil disturbance requires doctrine and guidelines that differ from those used to counter conventional forces and normally require detailed coordination with HN military, security, and police forces. More significantly, based on political, cultural, or other perspectives, activities that disrupt friendly operations may be perceived as legitimate by a large number of the local populace. **Countering Level I threats is considered to be part of the day-to-day FP measures implemented by all commanders.** Key to countering these threats is the active support of some portion of the civilian population, normally those sympathetic to US or multinational goals.

(2) **Level II Threats. Level II threats include small scale (described as less than company-sized equivalents) irregular forces conducting unconventional warfare that can pose serious threats to military forces and civilians.** These attacks can cause significant disruptions to military operations as well as the orderly conduct of local government and services. These forces are capable of conducting well coordinated, but small scale, hit and run attacks, IED and VBIED attacks, and ambushes and may include significant standoff weapons threats such as mortars, rockets, rocket propelled grenades, and SAMs. Level II threats may include special operations forces that are highly trained in unconventional warfare. These activities may also include operations typically associated with terrorist attacks outlined in the previous paragraph including air, land, and sea vehicle hijacking. These forces establish and activate espionage networks, collect intelligence, carry out specific sabotage missions, develop target lists, and conduct damage assessments of targets struck. They are capable of conducting raids and ambushes. If the JFC assigns a base boundary to an installation, sufficient organic forces must exist on that installation to deter and defeat Level II forces as defined.

(3) **Level III threats** may be encountered when a threat force has the capability of projecting combat power by air, land, or sea, anywhere into the operational area. Specific examples include airborne, heliborne, and amphibious operations; large combined arms ground force operations; and infiltration operations involving large numbers of individuals or small groups infiltrated into the operational area, regrouped at predetermined times and locations, and committed against priority targets. Air and missile threats to bases/base clusters and LOCs may also pose risks to joint forces, presenting themselves

with little warning time. **Level III threats necessitate a decision to commit a tactical combat force (TCF) or other significant available forces to counter the threat.** This threat level is beyond the capability of base and base cluster defense and response forces.

3. Joint Security Framework

a. **A JSA is a specific surface area designated to facilitate protection of bases.** Regional political considerations and sensitivities will influence whether a JSA is established. The JSA may be used in both linear and nonlinear operations. Figure I-2 depicts a notional organizational structure for JSO in which all bases are located in a land component commander's area of operations (AO).

b. The size of a JSA may vary considerably and is highly dependent on the size of the operational area, mission essential assets, logistic support requirements, threat, or scope of the joint operation. In linear operations the JSA may be included in, be separate from or adjoin the rear areas of the joint force land component commander (JFLCC) or joint force maritime component commander (JFMCC) or Service component commanders.

c. **JSAs may be designated where joint forces are engaged in combat operations or where stability operations are the primary focus.** Providing security of units, activities, bases/base clusters, and LOCs located in noncontiguous areas presents unique challenges based on the location, distance between supporting bases, and the security environment.

Providing security of units, activities, bases and/or base clusters, and lines of communications located in noncontiguous areas presents unique challenges.

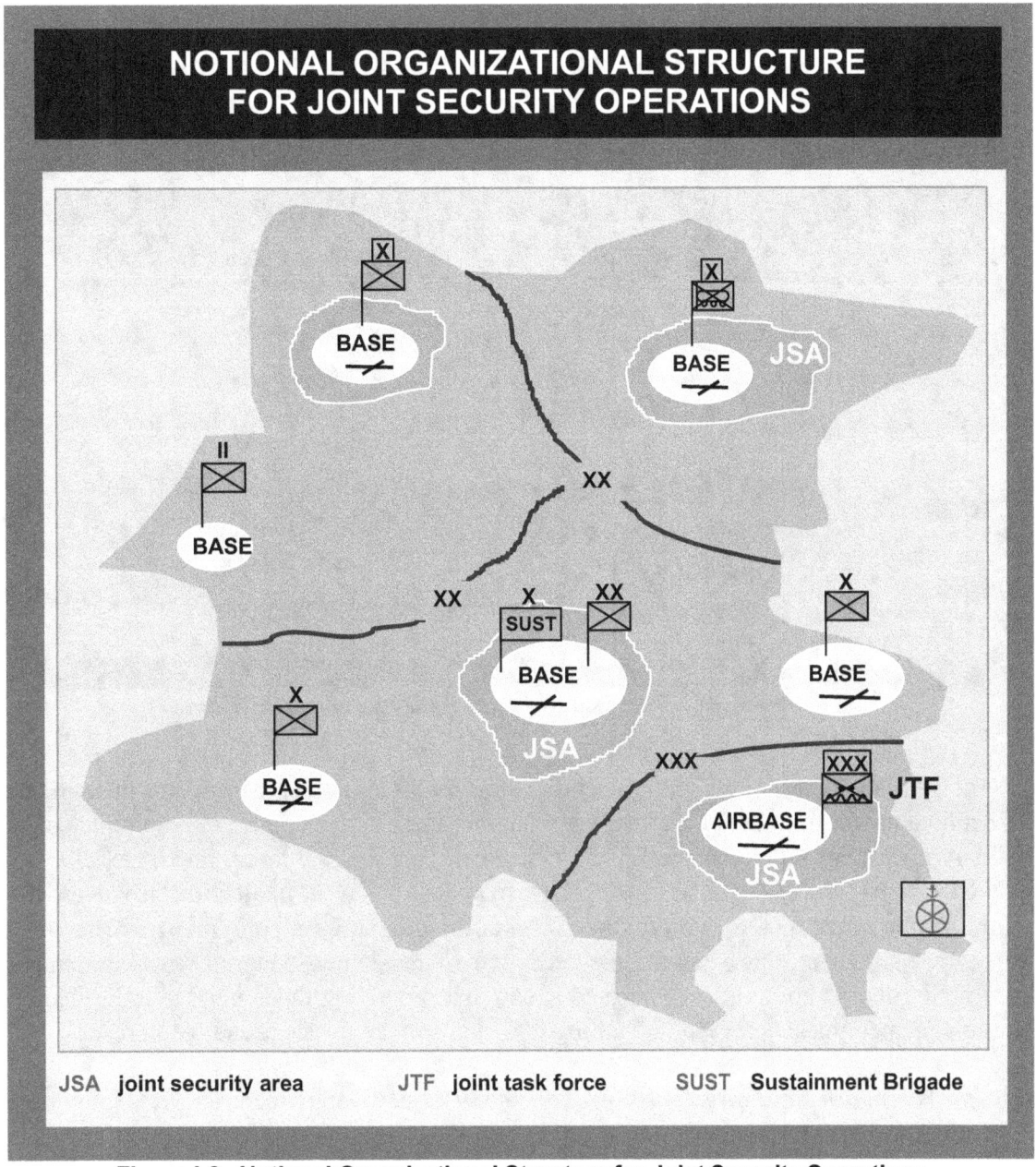

Figure I-2. Notional Organizational Structure for Joint Security Operations

d. JSAs may be established in different countries in the GCC's area of responsibility (AOR). The airspace above the JSA is normally not included in the JSA. This airspace is normally governed by procedures promulgated in JP 3-52, *Airspace Control*. The JSA will typically evolve as the operational area changes in accordance with (IAW) requirements to support and defend the joint force. A maritime amphibious objective area may precede a JSA when establishing a lodgment. A lodgment would normally be expanded to an area including existing ports and airfields from which bare base operations could be conducted, and then eventually evolve to areas including multiple countries and sea boundaries.

4. Base Functions and Nodes

Base functions and nodes include, but are not limited to **the items shown in Figure I-3 and described below.**

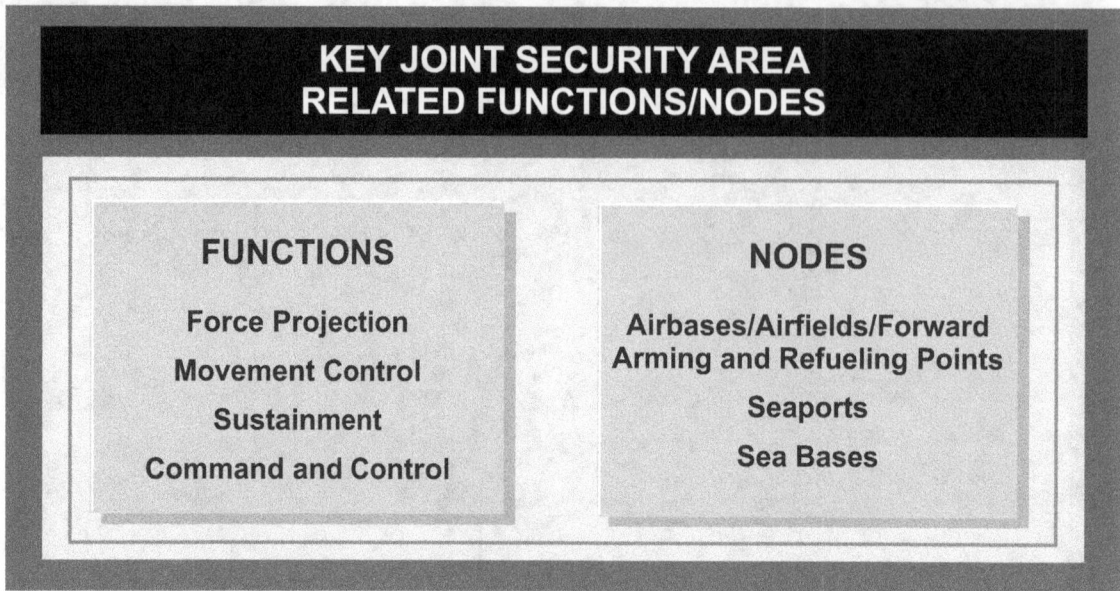

KEY JOINT SECURITY AREA RELATED FUNCTIONS/NODES

FUNCTIONS

Force Projection

Movement Control

Sustainment

Command and Control

NODES

Airbases/Airfields/Forward Arming and Refueling Points

Seaports

Sea Bases

Figure I-3. Key Joint Security Area Related Functions/Nodes

a. **Force Projection.** Force projection is the ability to project the military instruments of national power from the United States or another theater, in response to requirements for military operations. It allows the JFC to strategically concentrate forces and materiel to set the conditions for mission success. **The process of force projection involves the mobilization, deployment, employment, sustainment, and redeployment of the joint force.** A secure area is vital for the reception of personnel, materiel, and equipment; assembling them into units at designated staging sites; moving those units to a destination within the operational area; and integrating these units into a mission ready joint force.

For further information on force projection see JP 3-35, Deployment and Redeployment Operations.

b. **Movement Control.** Movement control is the planning, routing, scheduling, controlling and coordinating of responsibilities for personnel and cargo movement over LOCs throughout the operational area. Freedom of movement is critical to the support of the joint force and **joint movement control must be closely coordinated with JSO.** The JFC or subordinate JFC normally centralizes transportation movement by designating a joint movement center (JMC). The JMC controls intratheater force movement, coordinates strategic movements with US Transportation Command (USTRANSCOM) and oversees the execution of transportation priorities. Rail terminals, SPODs, APODs and other key transportation nodes may be located in a JSA.

For further information on movement control see JP 4-09, Distribution Operations.

c. **Sustainment.** The primary mission of many of the forces in a JSA is to sustain joint force operations and forces throughout the operational area. These forces may include any number and type of logistic units and include key supply, medical treatment facilities, and logistic capabilities provided by contractors. Where possible, medical treatment facilities should be situated away from all legitimate military targets to avoid endangerment. The Geneva Conventions prescribe the protections applicable to medical treatment facilities and their personnel.

For further information on sustainment see JP 4-0, Joint Logistics, *as well as other applicable 4-series joint publications.*

d. **Command and Control.** Bases containing C2 capabilities such as major headquarters and signal centers are critical installations in a JSA. The loss of this capability may have a significant impact on the entire operation.

e. **Air Bases, Airfields, Forward Arming and Refueling Points.** Airfields are critical nodes and are therefore lucrative targets for attack. **Aircraft approach and departure corridors and the immediate areas contiguous to the base from which threats to aircraft may originate are critically important and a challenging joint force security consideration.**

f. **Seaports.** SPODs, seaports of embarkation, and joint logistics over-the-shore sites are key nodes often located on a vulnerable seam between the land and naval force commander AOs. Therefore, component or subordinate joint force commanders must ensure advance coordination for security operations planning that entails C2, communications, rules of engagement (ROE), coordination points and responsibility for security along LOCs and employment of forces. The JFC and subordinate JFCs ensure that port security plans and responsibilities are clearly delineated and assigned.

g. **Sea Bases.** The JFMCC normally uses the composite warfare commander construct for defense of seabasing operations with principal warfare commanders establishing preplanned responses to defend the sea base, as well as sealift, airlift, and connector craft within the assigned geographical area. Proximity to the littorals, especially ports and harbors and the requirement to respond to threats along boundaries will be of interest to the JSC and may require close coordination between the two. The relationship between supported and supporting commanders, while similar to those described in Chapter II, "Command and Control," and Chapter IV, "Security of Bases and Base Clusters," are complicated by the multiple tasks that may be assigned to the individual ships. Environmental factors and the possibility that the shipping will not remain static may complicate defensive planning.

Intentionally Blank

CHAPTER II
COMMAND AND CONTROL

> *"Even in friendly territory a fortified camp should be set up; a general should never have to say: 'I did not expect it.'"*
>
> **The Emperor Maurice**
> **The Strategikon**
> **c. 600 AD**

1. Introduction

Unity of command is fundamental to effective security within the JSA. The JFC works toward this end by designating operational areas, selecting appropriate command structures, and establishing a C2 network through multinational, subordinate, and adjacent commanders to direct and coordinate the actions of components and supporting organizations or agencies. **C2 authority and responsibilities must be established for the units and activities throughout the operational area for the security of the bases and base clusters and their supporting LOCs.** Operations within the JSA will almost always involve interaction with a combination of HN forces, multinational forces (MNFs), contractor employees, noncombatants, US country teams, intergovernmental organizations (IGOs), and NGOs. This chapter discusses the roles and responsibilities, command relationships, operations centers, and requirements for JSO throughout an operational area.

2. Joint Security Operations Command and Control

a. **The JFC will normally designate JSAs to ensure the security of base/base clusters and LOCs.** The JFC establishes C2 relationships within the operational area, but may delegate certain authority to subordinate commanders in order to ensure effective C2 and to facilitate decentralized execution of security operations.

b. The JFC may retain control of JSO and may coordinate them through the operations directorate of a joint staff (J-3), or he may designate a functional or Service component commander with joint security responsibilities. To facilitate JSO, **commanders should establish a joint security element to coordinate JSO**. The individual who normally leads a joint security element is referred to as the JSC.

c. **The JSC (or staff element) may establish a joint security coordination center (JSCC)** using elements from the JSC's staff and representatives from all components operating in the operational area to assist in meeting joint security requirements. Component and staff representation will vary IAW mission, forces, and security requirements.

d. Bases/base clusters will normally be established to support joint operations and placed under the control of a base commander or base cluster commander. The base commander is responsible for security within the base boundary and has a direct interest in the security of the area surrounding the base. The area commander will establish base boundaries in coordination with (ICW) the base or base cluster commander. Base defense is accomplished in a coordinated effort by base defense forces providing security within the base boundary and other ground or surface forces executing security tasks outside that boundary. **The base boundary is not necessarily the base perimeter, rather it should be established based upon the factors of mission, enemy, terrain and weather, troops and support available — time available (METT-T), specifically balancing the need of the base defense forces to control key terrain with their ability to accomplish the mission.** Base boundaries may be dynamic, requiring ongoing coordination due to changing METT-T factors over time and host nation limitations.

e. The JFC may task the land, air, or maritime component commander to provide TCFs to counter Level III threats. The JFC also assesses the availability and effectiveness of HN contributions to base security. Based on this assessment, the JFC may be required to adjust the concept of operations, sequencing, and unit missions. Transportation (ports, highway networks, waterways, airfields, and railroads) nodes; C2, intelligence capabilities, and existing host-nation support (HNS) and civil considerations all impact how the JSA will be organized and operations conducted.

JOINT SECURITY AREA- 32D ARMY AIR AND MISSILE DEFENSE COMMAND OPERATION IRAQI FREEDOM EXPERIENCE

During the initial phases of Operation IRAQI FREEDOM, General Tommy Franks, Commander of US Central Command and coalition forces designated the land component commander (CFLCC), as the joint security coordinator for Kuwait and Northeast Saudi Arabia. He in turn designated the Commander, 32d Army Air and Missile Defense Command (32 AAMDC), as the CFLCC Deputy C3 to coordinate operational protection. 32 AAMDC reorganized and augmented it's staff with military police, chemical, engineer, and other key expertise, and served as the single point of contact integrating theater level operational protection efforts. Commander, 32 AAMDC recommended operational force protection priorities to the CJFLCC, led the joint security area (JSA) operational force protection board, oversaw high-value asset vulnerability assessments of JSA priorities, recommended protection measures needed to optimize the joint, interagency, and multinational force's protection stance, and monitored execution and risk mitigation of these measures. A coalition operational protection coordination center was also established under the 32d to further integrate Kuwaiti and coalition efforts. This operation highlighted the need for a single commander to standardize force protection conditions and to participate in joint protection working groups. The benefits of this structure included preventing a single dimensional approaches and ensuring that there were no seams in protection.

Various Sources

f. **The base commander is responsible for security operations** and will exercise tactical control (TACON) over all forces performing base defense missions within the base boundary. This includes both isolated bases and bases with a contiguous joint force area commander. The base/base cluster commander will coordinate such operations with the joint security element, HN SF, or other agencies as appropriate.

3. **Roles and Responsibilities**

   a. **US Embassy Representatives**

   (1) **Chief of Mission (COM).** The COM is responsible for the direction, coordination, and supervision of all US Government (USG) executive branch employees in that country (except those under the command of a US area military commander). GCC and COM security memorandums of agreement (MOAs) do not alter established command relationships, nor relieve commanders of responsibility for unit security. The GCC has responsibility for all Department of Defense (DOD) elements and personnel within that geographic AOR, except those for whom security responsibility has been transferred to the COM via the MOA process.

   (2) **Regional Security Officer (RSO).** The RSO is the COM's senior security officer and manages programs to assure the security functions of all US embassies and consulates in a given country or group of adjacent countries. The RSO works closely with the senior defense official/defense attaché (SDO/DATT) to ensure the safety and security of DOD elements and personnel for whom the COM has security responsibility.

   (3) **Senior Defense Official/Defense Attaché.** The SDO/DATT is the senior US military officer in a foreign country representing the Secretary of Defense (SecDef), the Chairman of the Joint Chiefs of Staff, and the GCC. Specific SDO/DATT responsibilities for JSO include, but are not limited to the following:

   (a) Function as the single point of contact for JSO for all DOD noncombatant command elements that are the security responsibility of the COM.

   (b) In designated countries, and IAW GCC/COM security MOAs, has FP responsibility for the in-country combatant command forces.

   (c) Coordinate with JSC on JSO issues.

   (d) Has authority over in-country noncombatant command forces in cases of emergency wherein US national/or DOD interests are involved and the urgency of the situation precludes referral up the chain of command to the GCC.

   (e) ICW the COM and RSO, initiate combined JSO planning with the HN and coordinate execution of these operations with the COM, GCC, through the JSC and ICW the JFC.

(f) Perform additional joint security responsibilities and duties as assigned by the GCC.

b. **Department of Defense**

(1) **Geographic Combatant Commander.** A GCC is ultimately responsible for all military JSO conducted in the AOR. The GCC, through the JSCC or similar organization, coordinates JSO through the SDO/DATT with the COM as appropriate. **GCCs establish AOR-wide FP measures, procedures, and policies for joint forces, family members, DOD civilian workforce, and designated government contractor employees that are assigned, attached, in-transit, or otherwise physically located within their AORs.** In addition, the GCCs provide support for interagency, IGO, NGO, and HN activities to enhance security for US forces, US citizens, and HN citizens. These responsibilities include maintaining the security of the command and protecting bases, LOCs, and critical HN infrastructure upon which the GCC depends against attack during on-going military operations. GCCs must ensure that subordinate staffs and/or commands are formally designated with the authority to conduct JSO.

(2) **Functional Combatant Commanders (CCDRs).** Elements of functional combatant commands providing support to the operational area, such as USTRANSCOM and US Special Operations Command, may establish facilities or occupy bases within the operational area. **The functional CCDR coordinates with the applicable GCC and/or subordinate JFC to ensure that these facilities or bases are adequately secured.** Command and coordination relationships between those elements and the area or base commanders subordinate to the JFC will be defined by orders or MOA. Coordination must include sharing of intelligence information, because supporting operations of functional CCDRs are often planned outside the operational area.

(3) **Subordinate Joint Force Commander.** Subordinate JFCs include the commanders of subordinate unified commands and joint task forces (JTFs). Subordinate JFCs have the authority to organize forces to best accomplish the assigned mission based on their concept of operations. Subordinate JFCs provide security of all military bases and LOCs within their joint operations area (JOA). The subordinate JFC conducts joint security planning, risk assessment, and force allocation; assigns AOs; and designates LOCs. They do this by either ensuring that the joint security coordination authority duties are clearly assigned to a formally designated JSC or embedding the authority in the J-3 staff.

(4) **Joint Security Coordinator.** Establishing and maintaining JSO throughout the operational area, although vital to the survivability and success of the joint force, **is an economy of force mission**. The JFC dedicates assets for JSO in proportion to the severity of the threat in order to conserve resources and prevent degradation of support. This function is normally vested in the JFC's staff or with a component commander with the capability to perform the function. In a low-threat environment, the JFC will normally designate JSC responsibilities within the joint staff (e.g., J-3). In this environment, the inherent defensive capabilities of bases, units, or HN forces are generally adequate to deter the threat. **In high-threat environments, the JFC normally designates a JSC to provide**

a dedicated focus on JSO within the JSA(s). Under these circumstances, the JFC normally designates a component commander with the appropriate capabilities and force structure to perform this function. The JFC considers mission requirements, force capabilities, the nature of the operating environment, and the threat in making the designation. Figures II-1 and II-2 depict notional operational area C2 networks, with options for the selection of the JSC.

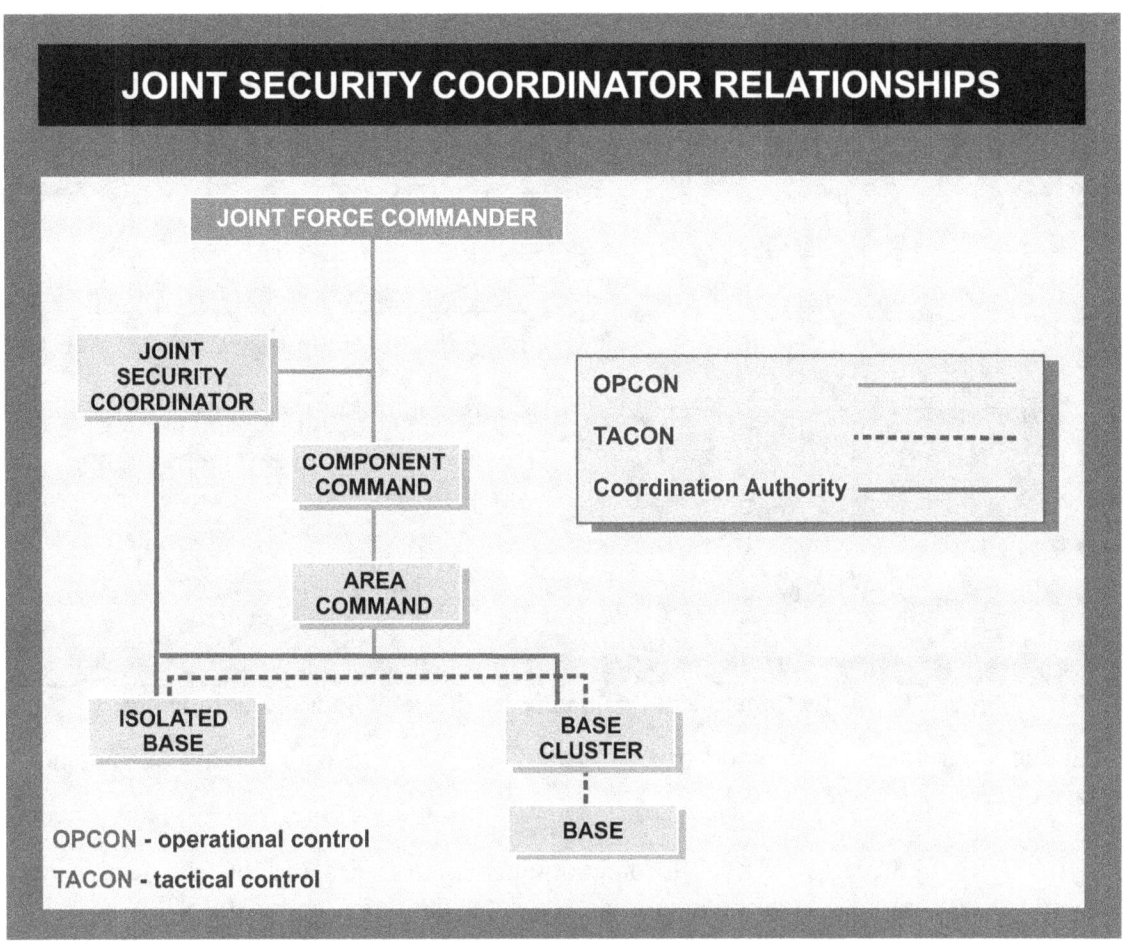

Figure II-1. Joint Security Coordinator Relationships

(a) **The JSC coordinates the overall security of the JSA(s) IAW JFC directives and priorities.** The JSC coordinates with appropriate commanders on security issues to facilitate sustainment, HNS, infrastructure development and protection, in addition to movements of the joint force. The JSC's overall coordination responsibility for security of the JSA(s) does not lessen the responsibility that component elements residing or operating in the operational area have for their own security. The JSC also assist commanders establish reliable intelligence support and practice terrain management within their operational area with due consideration of security requirements. The JSC establishes secure and survivable communications with all forces and commands operating in or transiting the JSA(s). The JSC normally coordinates security requirements and priorities

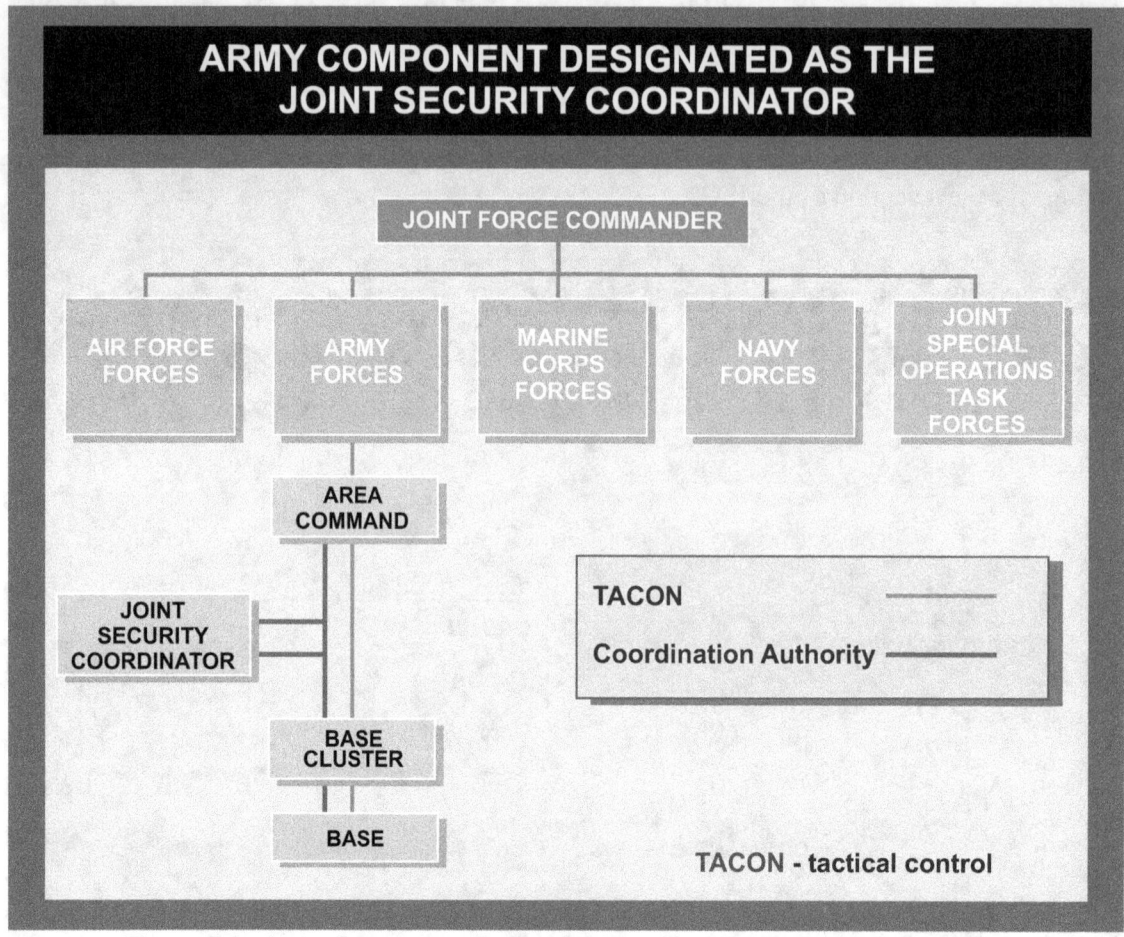

ARMY COMPONENT DESIGNATED AS THE JOINT SECURITY COORDINATOR

JOINT FORCE COMMANDER

AIR FORCE FORCES | ARMY FORCES | MARINE CORPS FORCES | NAVY FORCES | JOINT SPECIAL OPERATIONS TASK FORCES

AREA COMMAND

JOINT SECURITY COORDINATOR

BASE CLUSTER

BASE

TACON ————

Coordination Authority ————

TACON - tactical control

Figure II-2. Army Component Designated as the Joint Security Coordinator

with the joint force air component commander (JFACC)/area air defense commander (AADC).

(b) In cases of Level III threat or other emergencies, the JFC may designate a subordinate commander with the authority to counter the threat and restore JSA security. The JSC will support requests by the assigned commanders.

(c) Specific joint security coordination across the range of military operations includes coordinating with appropriate commanders and staff to ensure that the following applies:

1. The base and LOC construction and security posture in JSA supports the JFC's concept of operations and is adaptable to support future operations.

2. The overall base and LOC security plan is developed and coordinated with appropriate US forces, multinational forces, other US agencies, noncombatant command forces under the COM and SDO/DATT, and HN commands.

3. The chain of command established by the JFC and the degree of authority granted to the JSC are adequate for the mutual protection and security of all US personnel and assets in the operational area.

4. The intelligence, counterintelligence (CI), and law enforcement networks are responsive to the needs of base commanders and LOC security forces operating in the JSA.

5. Objective criteria are developed and shared for assessing the criticality and vulnerability of bases, base clusters, LOCs, and key infrastructure, both internal and external to the operational area, to prioritize security improvements and position mobile security forces (MSFs) and TCFs (as required).

6. Coordination with the JFACC/AADC has been completed to ensure that air and missile defense requirements for the JSA(s) are integrated into US, multinational, and/or HN air defense plans IAW JFC priorities and concept of operations.

7. Base and LOC defense plans incorporate adequate provisions and procedures for CBRN warning and reporting procedures.

8. Appropriate liaison is established with multinational and HN commands for coordination of JSO.

9. All relevant international and domestic (US and HN) legal guidelines impacting on security within the JSA (such as HNS agreements, law of armed conflict guidance, status-of-forces agreements [SOFAs], and ROE) are disseminated and shared to appropriate command levels.

(5) **Component Commanders.** The JFC normally exercises command through Service or functional component commanders and designates command responsibilities based on the operational mission.

(a) **Security Responsibilities**

1. Component commanders with area responsibilities provide for the defense of their AOs, the overall defense of bases located in their AOs, and for LOCs within their AOs.

2. Within established AOs, other component commanders must ensure and provide for the defense of their assets and/or bases critical to their component responsibilities. A component commander with unique security requirements (for example, those related to the shoulder-launched SAM footprint around a joint operating base) should expect to provide the majority of forces for the defense of those assets/bases.

3. When an area of operation is not established, commanders must provide for the defense of those bases critical to their component responsibilities.

Accordingly, that component should expect to provide the majority of forces to conduct these security operations.

(b) Joint security responsibilities are usually modified by HN agreements when operating in the sovereign territory of multinational partners who normally retain responsibility for the overall security of an operational area. In these circumstances, the component commanders would continue to execute their security authority as directed by the JFC through other appropriate commanders and **ICW the JSC**, to include the following:

1. Organizing appropriate component bases into base clusters and designating base and base cluster commanders. Organizing the defense of bases within their operational area.

2. Coordinating the local security of bases and base clusters, LOCs, and key infrastructure to include establishing priorities for security and area damage control (ADC) IAW JFC directives.

3. Establishing a C2 network linking bases and base clusters, and ensuring that adequate coordination is established with MNFs and HN activities within or bordering their security zones.

4. Ensuring that base and base cluster defense plans are adequate, coordinated, and complementary to applicable HN security plans.

5. Serving as the single point of contact for coordinating JSO within their AO with the HN (if so designated by the JFC).

6. Ensuring that base or LOC MSFs as well as other area security units are identified, trained, and positioned IAW JFC directives and priorities.

7. Performing other security responsibilities as directed by the JFC through the JSC.

(c) Service and functional component commanders may also establish bases IAW JFC guidance to meet the JFC's objectives. In this case, component commanders delegate authority to provide security and defense of those bases to the base commander and coordinate security and defense issues with Service or functional components with area responsibilities, as appropriate.

(6) **Area Commanders.** **Service component commanders with area responsibilities** establish base and base clusters within their AOs and delegate the authority to provide security to those subordinate commanders.

(a) **Component commanders, most typically the Army or Marine Corps commanders with a JSA in their AO may be designated as the JSC and be delegated**

with the authority to conduct security operations. In lower-level threat environments, the commander, Army forces may delegate joint security coordination responsibilities to a major Army logistic unit, normally a theater support command (TSC). The TSC would subdivide and assign specific security areas to its subordinate sustainment brigades. Army TSCs and sustainment brigades would be responsible to plan, coordinate, control, and execute JSO within the JSA.

(b) The JSA or a designated part of the operational area may be the responsibility of the commander, Marine Corps forces (COMMARFOR). The COMMARFOR may designate to the commander of the Marine air-ground task force (MAGTF) the JSO mission, including the defense of logistic and air bases within the JSA. The MAGTF commander may, in turn, choose to designate the MAGTF logistics combat element commander for this mission. Tasks may include joint security responsibilities (e.g., area damage control, convoy security, movement control) that will be conducted by Marine Corps forces in the JSA.

(7) **Base Cluster Commander.** When necessary, the JFC may designate a senior base commander as a base cluster commander. A base cluster is a collection of bases, geographically grouped for mutual protection and ease of C2. The base cluster commander is responsible for coordinating the defense of bases within the base cluster and for integrating defense plans of bases into a base cluster defense plan. The base cluster commander normally has **TACON of forces assigned to the base primarily for the purpose of local base defense. The authority the base cluster commander will exercise over other forces residing on the base for primary purposes other than local base**

For base defense purposes, the base commander typically exercises tactical control over forces assigned or attached to the base.

defense must be established by the JFC and be explicitly detailed in order that appropriate JSO may occur as part of the overall base defense plan.

(8) **Base Commander.** The JFC normally designates the commander of the primary occupant of a base as the base commander. The base commander is responsible for all base security operations within the base boundary and will closely coordinate operations with all occupants. A base commander provides and **exercises base defense C2 through a base defense operations center (BDOC).** The base commander establishes a BDOC to serve as the focal point for force protection, security and defense within the base boundary. Through the BDOC, the base commander plans, directs, integrates, coordinates, and controls all base defense efforts, and coordinates and integrates security operations with the base cluster operations center (BCOC) as appropriate. This normally involves **TACON over forces assigned or attached to the base primarily for the purpose of local base defense.** The base commander may also exercise TACON over **other forces residing on the base for primary purposes other than local base defense** when these forces are called on to perform functions related to base defense or local security missions as part of the overall base defense plan. Commanders of units residing on the base that are not explicitly detailed by the JFC for base defense should coordinate with the base commander for participation in the base defense plan. The base commander provides for base terrain management and the location of all critical assets. **The base commander is determined by the JFC based on the classification of the base and by the functions and unique security requirements of the individual Services. The Service designated with base command responsibilities provides the C2 structure for FP, security, and defense operations within the base boundary.**

(9) **Tenant Unit Commanders.** Tenant unit commanders are commanders of units that reside and operate on, but do not fall under the direct command of the base commander. **Tenant unit commanders must actively participate in the preparation of base security and defense plans.** They will normally be required to provide security of their own forces and high-value assets, provide individuals to perform perimeter/gate security, and will often be assigned battle positions IAW base security plans. These forces, when provided, will generally be under the TACON of the base commander for the purpose of base defense. Most importantly, **they are required to ensure that all personnel are properly trained to support and participate in base security in the event of attack.** Tenant joint special operations task forces, because of low personnel densities, must coordinate the above requirements with the base commander (see Figure II-3).

(10) **Tactical Combat Force Commanders.** In operations where there is the possibility of a Level III threat, the JFC may elect to establish a dedicated joint security combat force called a TCF. **The command relationships between the TCF and subordinate commanders will be determined by the JFC.** The TCF is normally commanded by a designated land component commander or subordinate commander. The TCF is a combat unit, with appropriate combat support and combat service support assets, which is assigned the mission of defeating Level III threats. The threat requiring the commitment of a TCF is usually of such magnitude that several bases or base clusters are threatened. Once committed, the TCF is given an operational area by the appropriate

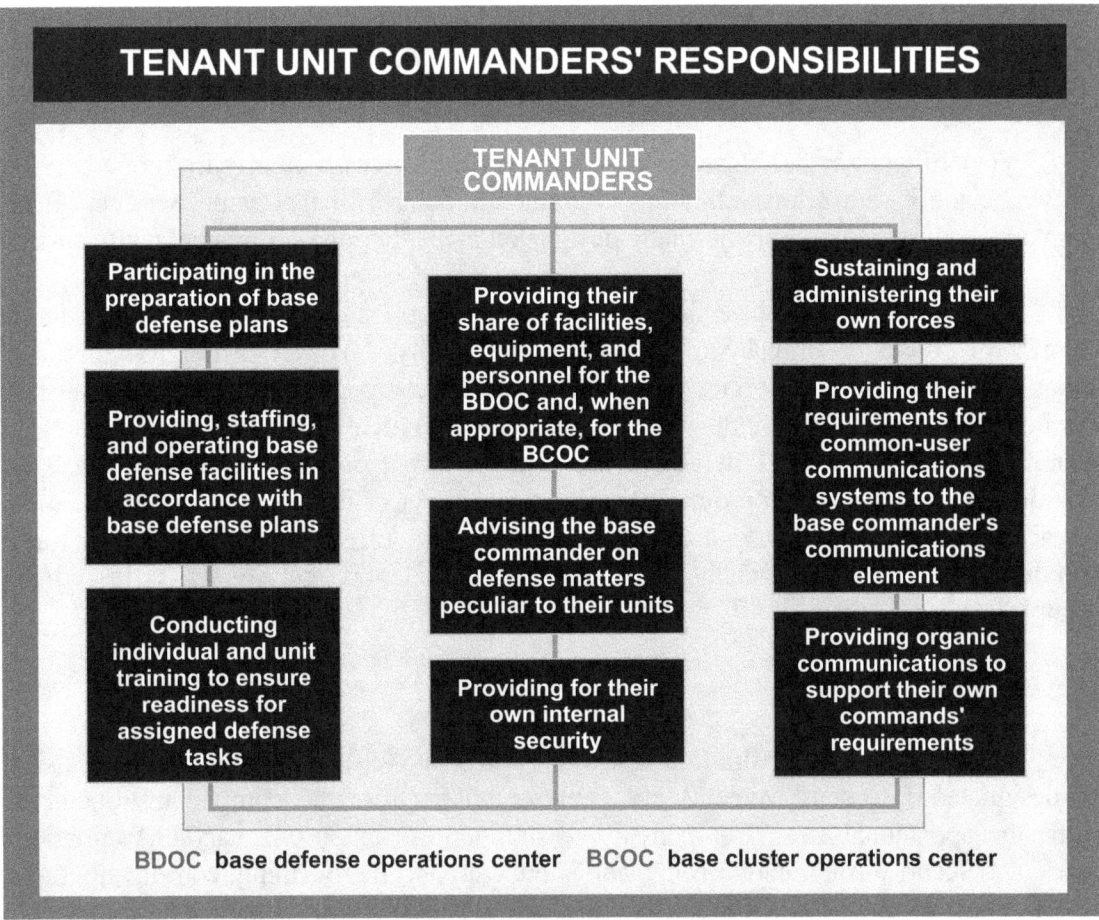

TENANT UNIT COMMANDERS' RESPONSIBILITIES

TENANT UNIT COMMANDERS

- Participating in the preparation of base defense plans
- Providing, staffing, and operating base defense facilities in accordance with base defense plans
- Conducting individual and unit training to ensure readiness for assigned defense tasks
- Providing their share of facilities, equipment, and personnel for the BDOC and, when appropriate, for the BCOC
- Advising the base commander on defense matters peculiar to their units
- Providing for their own internal security
- Sustaining and administering their own forces
- Providing their requirements for common-user communications systems to the base commander's communications element
- Providing organic communications to support their own commands' requirements

BDOC base defense operations center   BCOC base cluster operations center

Figure II-3. Tenant Unit Commanders' Responsibilities

commander in which to accomplish its assigned mission. With this operational area, the TCF commander is the supported commander for the integration and synchronization of maneuver, fires, and interdiction. This may require the rearrangement of boundaries within an operational area. Plans for the employment of the TCF should be coordinated and rehearsed with area commanders, base cluster commanders, base commanders and with the HN.

4. **Establishment of Base and Base Cluster Command Relationships**

a. **Command Relationships in Joint Security Operations.** The JFC, normally through a designated JSC, ensures that appropriate command relationships among subordinate area, base and base cluster commanders are established and understood by all affected commands. Command relationships determine the interrelated responsibilities between commanders as well as the authority of commanders in the chain of command. **The typical command relationships established in support of JSO should be TACON between the base or base cluster commander and the dedicated security force, when the attached force is from a different component command.**

b. **Base Classification.** Unless determined by higher authority, the JFC will determine the classification of bases IAW established policies. A base may be either a single Service base or a joint base.

(1) **Single Service Base.** A base that contains forces primarily from one Service and where the base's primary mission is under the control of that same Service. Base commanders of these bases are normally designated by the Service component commander.

(2) **Joint Base.** A base that has two or more Service units where no Service has a majority of forces or primacy of mission responsibility. The JFC assigns command authority of this base to a Service component and that component will then designate the base commander. When a joint base is designated, **it is critically important that the JFC, normally through the JSC, delegates the authority to conduct JSO within the base boundary to a single commander**. However, other Services have SF that contribute to or can accept command of base or base cluster security (elements of the Navy's Navy Expeditionary Combat Command and US Coast Guard port security units [PSUs] for example).

5. Operations Centers

a. **Joint Security Coordination Center.** A JFC may elect to establish a JSCC using the designated JSC staff elements and representatives from the components operating within the operational area. Component and staff representation will vary IAW mission, forces, and security zone requirements, and should support the planning, coordination, and execution of all joint security related operations. The JSC will ensure that component representation and representation from the JSC staff is sufficient to support assigned mission responsibilities. **The JSCC serves as the JSC's full time centralized planning, coordinating, monitoring, advising, and directing agency for operational area JSO.** It coordinates with other elements on the JSC staff, with higher, lower, and adjacent command staffs, and with HN and allied command staffs. The JSCC is manned with full time staff for key personnel and additional "as needed" personnel with subject matter expertise as available.

See Appendix A, "Joint Security Operations Centers," for more information on the functions and organization of the JSCC.

b. **Rear Area Operations and Rear Tactical Operations Centers.** Army and Marine Corps area and subarea commanders usually have rear area operations centers (RAOCs) and rear tactical operations centers (RTOCs) to assist in accomplishing their area security and defense mission. These C2 facilities serve as the area and subarea commander's planning, coordinating, monitoring, advising and directing agencies for JSO. RAOCs may be designated as a JSCC and either RAOCs or RTOCs can serve as BDOCs and/or BCOCs.

c. **Base Cluster Operations Center.** A BCOC is a C2 facility established by the base cluster commander to serve as the focal point for the security of the bases within the base cluster. It plans, directs, integrates, coordinates, and controls all base cluster security efforts. The BCOC personnel keep the base cluster commander informed of the situation and resources available to cope with security related requirements. They coordinate all BDOC efforts, and integrates JSO with other designated higher-level staff as designated by the JFC. The nature of the BCOC depends on the combination of forces involved and may include other sister Services, multinational HN and/or other US agencies personnel. **The BCOC is similar in many respects to the land force unit's tactical operations center** and, in some cases, may be one and the same. Representatives from intelligence, maneuver, and fire support staff the BCOC. The base cluster commander provides other functional staff representatives to augment his base commanders as necessary. Multi-Service, other agency, HN and/or multinational representation should be part of the BCOC when elements of their armed forces, police, or paramilitary forces are directly involved in the overall base defense effort or they are a major tenant organization to the base.

See Appendix A, "Joint Security Operations Centers" for more information on the functions and organization of the BCOC.

   d. **Base Defense Operations Center.** A BDOC is a C2 facility established by the base commander as the focal point for FP, security, and defense within the base boundary. Through the BDOC, the base commander plans, directs, integrates, coordinates, and controls all base security efforts, and coordinates and integrates area security operations with the base cluster operations center (if established) or other designated higher-level staff as designated by the JSC. The nature of the BDOC depends on the combination of forces involved and may include sister Services, multinational HN and/or other US agencies personnel, depending on the combination of forces located at each particular base. Multi-Service, other agency, HN and/or multinational representation should be part of the BDOC when elements of their armed forces, police, or paramilitary forces are directly involved in the overall base defense effort or they are a major tenant organization to the base. The center normally consists of three primary sections —command, intelligence, and operations — with additional sections as deemed necessary. These additional sections could include a logistic section to plan the provision of services and support to the base, and an ADC section that provides inspection, planning, and control of the base's emergency response/ADC resources. The BDOC is manned full time with key personnel and augmented with subject matter expertise as required.

See Appendix A, "Joint Security Operations Centers," for more information on the functions and organization of the BDOC.

Intentionally Blank

CHAPTER III
PLANNING

"Never break the neutrality of any port or place, but never consider as neutral any place from whence an attack is allowed to be made."

Horatio Nelson
Letter of Instruction
1804

1. Introduction

The JSC, through the joint force subordinate commanders, base cluster commanders and base commanders, monitors and coordinates the overall organization and control of forces responsible for base and LOC security and advises the JFC on all issues associated with JSO. These forces must be trained, organized and equipped to properly execute JSO. This chapter sets forth joint force security planning considerations along with the discussion on special considerations relevant to JSO.

2. The Fundamentals of Planning Joint Security Operations

Understanding the basic planning fundamentals of JSO is key to the proper execution of this challenging mission. Commanders in the field should ensure security operations are being planned and executed as part of "normal" operations. The fundamentals of JSO planning are listed in Figure III-1.

FUNDAMENTALS OF JOINT SECURITY OPERATIONS PLANNING

- **Establish Clear Joint Security Related Command and Control Relationships and Responsibilities**

- **Understand the Enemy**

- **See the Operational Environment**

- **Use Defenders' Advantages**

- **Mitigate Defenders' Disadvantages**

- **Balance Security Actions With Civil and Political Considerations**

Figure III-1. Fundamentals of Joint Security Operations Planning

---

a. **Establish Clear Joint Security Related Command and Control Relationships and Responsibilities.** Key to proper joint security planning, coordination and execution is the establishment by the JFC or his designated representative of clear and well-understood C2 responsibilities. The JFC, normally assisted by a designated JSC, must ensure that base, base cluster, and LOC security C2 responsibilities are established early on in the decision-making process.

b. **Understand the Enemy.** Joint forces must **be familiar with the capabilities of enemy forces; weapons; equipment; tactics; and political, ideological, cultural, economic, and/or other motivational factors**. The status of the civilian populace as related to previous enemy activity may also play a significant role. Everyone from the base commander through the JFC must have access to the latest intelligence concerning probable enemy intent.

c. **See the Operational Environment.** Joint intelligence preparation of the operational environment (JIPOE) provides the commander a continuous, integrated, and comprehensive analysis of enemy capabilities, the anticipated impact on friendly operations and civilian populace, terrain, weather, and any other characteristics of the battlespace that may influence the JSC's decision. It helps the commander anticipate battlespace events, develop priority intelligence requirements (PIRs) and information requirements tied to those events, and develop effective counters to those events.

d. **Use the Defenders' Advantages.** There is strength in the defense and commanders and planners should take these advantages into account as they prepare and execute JSO. Key advantages to the defense include:

(1) The ability to fight from cover and concealment.

(2) Detailed knowledge of local waterways, terrain, and environment.

(3) The ability to prepare positions, routes between them, obstacles, and fields of fire in advance.

(4) The ability to plan communications, control measures, indirect fires, close air and logistic support to fit any predictable situation.

(5) The ability to conduct rehearsals of contingency response plans on the terrain they will be executed on.

e. **Mitigate Defenders' Disadvantages. Military bases and surface LOCs are fixed, often lucrative targets with limited depth for maneuver.** Mitigating the disadvantages of securing fixed facilities and LOCs is critical to the success of JSO. Key methods and techniques to mitigate these disadvantages include:

(1) Establish strongly defended boundaries with well-controlled access points.

(2) Integrate MSFs into base and LOC security plans.

(3) Apply aggressive countermeasures to include patrolling, observation posts (OPs), listening posts, etc., throughout the operational environment.

(4) Harden facilities and critical resources.

(5) Synchronize fires with base defense and LOC security actions.

(6) Conduct execution rehearsals.

(7) Develop, maintain, and execute CBRN emergency response measures.

(8) Integrate intelligence, surveillance, and reconnaissance (ISR) assets and other early detection assets to see beyond the base perimeter.

f. **Balance Security Actions with Civil and Political Considerations.** Base and LOC security will have to be planned and executed IAW the standing ROE/standing rules for the use of force (RUF) and other higher headquarters orders, which may include numerous constraints and restraints. All commanders and staff officers responsible for planning, coordinating, and executing JSO must take these factors into account. Failure to do so may have significant, possibly negative, strategic-level impact. Base commanders and their subordinates must comply with established ROE and should ensure that inconsistencies among Service components, multinational partners, and possibly even contractor personnel ROE are reconciled. Discrepancies need to be resolved at the JFC's level to ensure all bases and Services are operating with the same guidance. In areas with US country teams, commanders must liaise closely with COM through the SDO during planning efforts to account for all political considerations.

3. **Joint Security Operations Planning Overview**

Base and LOC security should be governed by the METT-T factors. Additionally, careful consideration should be given to the support available and to civil and political considerations.

a. **Mission. The primary mission of the base is to support joint force objectives.** Inherent in this mission is the subsidiary mission of securing these bases and LOCs from enemy action. The stated security plan should specify the following essential elements:

(1) Who will secure the base?

(2) Where each unit is positioned?

(3) When and for how long the unit must be prepared to provide security?

(4) What are the control and coordinating measures?

(5) What specifically the unit will secure – careful consideration should be given to the protection of any key assets within a given base or LOC related assets?

For more detailed guidance on planning see JP 5-0, Joint Operation Planning.

b. **Enemy.** Every intelligence and CI resource available to the base commander should be used to **determine enemy capabilities and intentions**.

The intelligence process and intelligence support to joint operations are discussed in JP 2-01, Joint and National Intelligence Support to Military Operations.

(1) **The JFC should provide commander's critical information requirements (CCIRs) to the staff and components.** CCIRs comprise a comprehensive list of information requirements identified by the commander as being critical in facilitating timely information management and the decision-making process that affect successful mission accomplishment. In the course of mission analysis, the intelligence planner identifies the intelligence required to answer the CCIRs. Mission analysis leads to the development of intelligence requirements (general or specific subjects upon which there is a need for the collection of information or the production of intelligence). **Those intelligence requirements deemed most important to mission accomplishment are identified by the commander as PIRs.** Based on the command's intelligence requirements, the intelligence staff develops more specific questions known as information requirements (those items of information that must be collected and processed to develop the intelligence required by the commander). **Those information requirements that are most critical or that would answer** a PIR are known as essential elements of information. Specific joint security related PIRs may include:

(a) The enemy's tactical, operational, and strategic objectives and intentions as they relate to attacks on bases and LOCs.

(b) Organization, size, and composition of forces, and locations of strongholds that threaten bases and LOCs.

(c) Movement of enemy personnel and equipment.

(d) Enemy intelligence capabilities to include use of local hire base workers, infiltrators.

(e) Enemy capabilities and tactics (special consideration should be given to standoff weapon capabilities such as mortars, theater missiles, SAMs, and CBRN materials).

(f) Local support for enemy cause.

(2) **Information requirements** deal with necessary information about the enemy, environment, and other factors that needs to be collected and processed in order to meet the intelligence and other requirements of the commanders responsible for JSO. The intelligence effort should be directed toward planning and direction, collection, processing and exploitation, analysis and production, and dissemination and integration of intelligence that will permit the development of friendly capabilities to:

(a) Prevent and disrupt enemy attacks on bases and LOCs.

(b) Counter enemy fires, mobility, electronic warfare, imagery, and human intelligence (HUMINT) capabilities.

(c) Identify and defend against enemy intelligence collection efforts.

In analyzing base security, commanders must consider observation and fields of fire, cover and concealment, obstacles, key terrain, and avenues of approach.

c. **Terrain and Weather. Bases and surface LOCs are usually selected in order to accomplish missions related to their use.** Although defensive considerations are frequently secondary, they must not be ignored. The nature of air bases, for example, precludes establishment of tight boundaries with extensive cover and concealment for defenders. However, the defense of an air base can be enhanced if the location does not allow the enemy to approach unobserved. Likewise, ports are located in or adjacent to urban areas. **Nonetheless, the base commander must make the best use of the terrain within the operational area.** Commanders analyzing terrain must consider all its military aspects, from the standpoints of base and LOC function as well as security considerations from both a defender's and enemy's perspective. Security considerations include observation and fields of fire, cover and concealment, obstacles, key terrain, and avenues of approach. Additionally, commanders must analyze how the weather affects both defender and enemy weapons systems and tactics. **Weather and visibility conditions can have a significant impact on land, air, and maritime operations.** Additionally, prevailing winds can determine the effectiveness of enemy employment of CBRN weapons and/or the release of toxic industrial materials from nearby industrial facilities. Commanders should minimize their own vulnerabilities to adverse weather conditions and exploit any advantages over enemy vulnerabilities.

d. **Troops and Support Available for Joint Security Operations.** There may be some units on a base whose primary missions are defense and security, such as military police (MP) at a large headquarters, SF on an air base, and air and missile defense forces. In some cases, the JFC or subordinate commander may determine that land combat forces, usually platoon to battalion task force level, may also be assigned as dedicated base, surface LOC and/or area defense forces. **In other cases, particularly bases where there are limited combat forces, security forces may be formed from logistic, transiting units, or other support units.** In these situations, support in the form of special training and equipment will be required. This support is essential in ensuring that such forces are capable of performing the required security missions and tasks. **Most on-call personnel made available for joint security related missions will be obtained from the units whose primary mission is not security-related.** In many cases, these personnel will not have the same degree of combat skills as dedicated security forces and therefore must receive additional training in marksmanship, tactics, and basic ground combat skills. Integration of these forces into successful JSO requires close supervision and leadership. Dedicated resources, normally from within the base, will be required to provide the needed support to ensure forces are at the requisite level to respond effectively. Figure III-2 shows troop capability requirements for each threat level.

(1) **Level I Threat Troop Requirements.** Level I threats involve day-to-day security measures that must be maintained by all military forces. At this level, **available assets should be able to detect and defeat enemy activities. Level I security activities are conducted primarily by the forces assigned to the mission, usually as tasks in addition to their primary duties**. Early in the process of planning for any joint security operation the JSC and unit commanders must determine which units and/or individuals will be exempt from security duties and ensure that those assigned security duties have the requisite ground combat skills to accomplish the mission. The JSC normally establishes a dedicated security force and determines its size and composition by striking a balance between economy of force requirements weighed against the enemy threat and the size and importance of the base or LOC.

(2) **Level II Threat Troop Requirements.** Level II threats include threats that will often require, in addition to the standard base and LOC self-security forces, a dedicated MSF or area command combat force specifically focused on JSO. The MSF would normally be, at a minimum, an MP platoon or SF flight, but may be a land force combat arms unit. Key capabilities of this force normally would include:

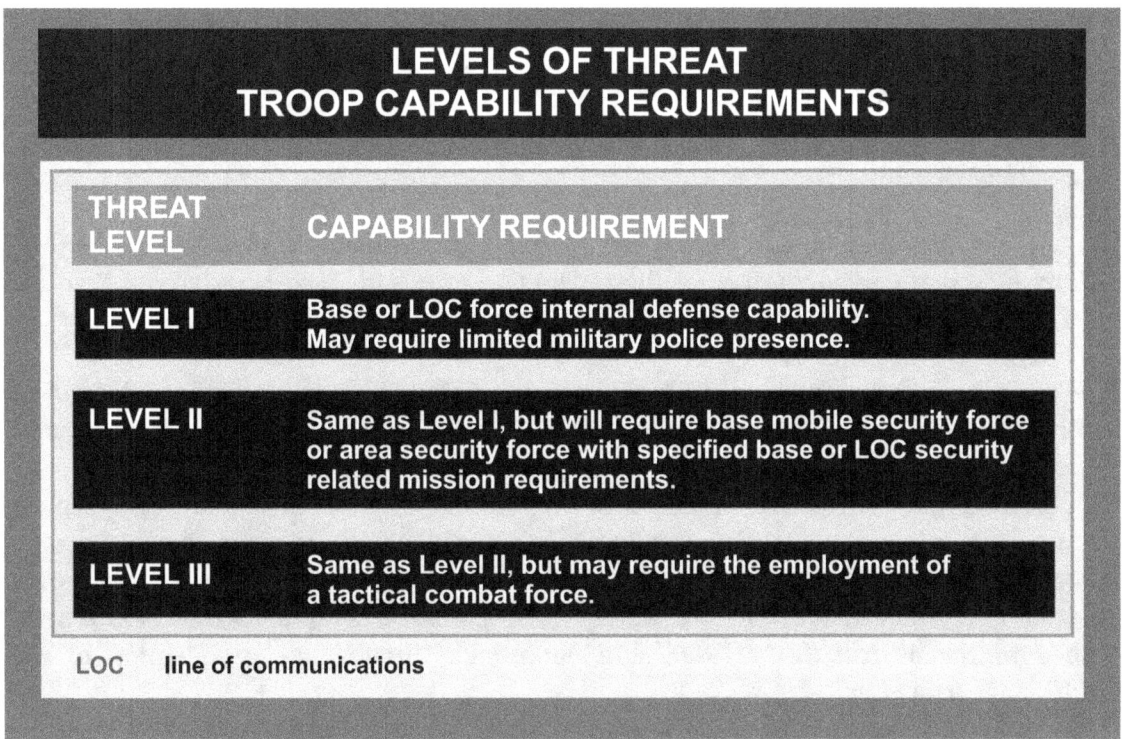

Figure III-2. Levels of Threat Troop Capability Requirements

(a) Armored mobility (armored wheeled or combat tracked vehicles).

(b) Larger caliber direct fire weapons (heavy machine guns, automatic grenade launcher, and/or direct fire cannons).

(c) Organic or on-call indirect fire capability (medium mortars at a minimum).

(3) **Level III Threat Troop Requirements.** Level III threats require the same forces as level II threats and normally include a TCF. A TCF is an on-call mobile response force capable of responding to larger-scale conventional or counterinsurgency threats in the JSA. A TCF normally consists of a combined arms task force with organic combat and combat support elements and ability to call for fires (indirect and air delivered).

e. **Time Available.** Commanders assess the time available for planning, preparing, and executing the mission. They consider how friendly or adversary forces will use the time and the possible results. Proper use of the time available can fundamentally alter the situation. Time available is normally defined in terms of the missions and tasks assigned and bounded by adversary capabilities. Commanders must use the time available effectively and provide subordinates with time to plan and prepare their own operations.

f. **Civil and Political Considerations.** JFC and subordinate planners must give significant consideration to the civil and political impact of joint security measures and actions. For example, closing key surface LOCs (military use highways, pipelines, rail ways, waterways) to civilian use may be desirable from a security perspective, but the potential impact on the local population and on relief and reconstruction programs could greatly outweigh the advantages of such measures.

4. Common Planning Considerations

a. **Force Protection.** Countering level I threats **is considered to be a part of the day-to-day FP measures for bases**. Antiterrorism (AT) measures will be a large part of the base security plan.

For more specific guidance on AT planning and operations requirements see JP 3-07.2, Antiterrorism, as well as the applicable GCC's FP and AT directives or operation orders.

b. **Intelligence.** Effective intelligence support, merged with CI and law enforcement agency information, is essential to conducting successful JSO. Current intelligence and CI estimates should be focused on joint security challenges and must incorporate intelligence from all US, multinational, and HN sources. **JSO must be completely and deliberately linked to the overall JFC JIPOE and component intelligence preparation of the battlespace processes.**

(1) **Responsibilities.** The JSC is responsible for coordinating the intelligence and CI requirements of organizations with JSO responsibilities with the intelligence directorate of a joint staff (J-2). The J-2, through the joint intelligence operations center (JIOC) and/or the joint intelligence support element (JISE), is responsible for ensuring that the appropriate resources and operations are allocated to support these requirements.

(2) **Intelligence Considerations.** The JSC requires timely and accurate all-source intelligence in order to coordinate appropriate joint security related actions; however, intelligence will typically come from supporting CI elements operating throughout the operational area and the supporting JIOC and/or JISE which may be able to provide surveillance video, imagery, and signals intelligence as required. Logistic units are also a lucrative source of information regarding potential unconventional, subversive, IEDs, CBRN, guerrilla, and terrorist threats. This information is usually reported through CI and operational channels simultaneously. The JSC, in conjunction with the combatant command counterintelligence support officer (CISO) or JTF CI coordination authority, will coordinate with appropriate commanders and staff to ensure:

(a) Reporting means and procedures are established and used for the timely reporting of suspicious activities or incidents to the JSC.

(b) Adequate liaison is established with HN military commands and government agencies in the operational area to collect valuable information from those sources.

(c) Chains of command are used to convey essential information and intelligence to support all forces engaged in JSO.

(d) Separate or transient forces that may have been diverted from other tasks, and which may not otherwise have access to critical information, receive effective intelligence support.

(3) **Counterintelligence.** An effective CI process is one of the most important ways that commanders and the JSC can contribute to maintaining adequate joint security. The CI process includes the complementary functions of investigations; operations; collection, reporting, and analysis; production, and dissemination. The J-2, through the CISO and in conjunction with the Service supporting CI organizations, should develop a CI plan for collection requirements, liaison operations with HN intelligence and security services, incident investigations, and analytical support, particularly to the JSC staff and the JSC force protection working group (FPWG) (if established). The CI plan should include an assessment of all foreign intelligence services. CI is particularly effective in assisting commanders, the JSC, and staffs in identifying the espionage, sabotage, subversion, and terrorist threats to bases and LOCs. CI can provide commands and staff with identification and analysis of threats from unconventional forces, terrorist, partisans, and civilian groups sympathetic to the adversary. The CISO is responsible for providing the commander with current CI estimates that include analysis of adversary or other foreign intelligence capabilities and other threats as appropriate. The CISO must ensure that effective communications networks and liaison with HNs, allies, joint forces, and law enforcement agencies are established and that this information is reported in a timely and consolidated manner to the impacted components responsible for planning and executing JSO.

More information on intelligence operations can be found in JP 2-0, Joint Intelligence.

c. **Communications**

(1) **General.** The JSC must have an interoperable, secure, reliable, flexible, and survivable communications network in order to accomplish the mission. Existing military or commercial communications systems should be used based on security and reliability to the maximum extent possible. However, additional communications systems (e.g., Joint World-Wide Intelligence Communications Systems) may be required to reconfigure or expand the network.

(2) **Communications System Support Responsibilities.** The joint force communications system directorate (J-6), ICW the JSC, provides overall management of organic communication system (e.g., single channel radios and internal switching or terminal equipment supporting the JSC staff) and coordinates with the appropriate system manager for nonorganic communications system support. The JSC will designate units to establish HN connectivity as required. (NOTE: The JSC will establish necessary liaison with the J-6 to ensure that all communications requirements for the JSA are met.)

(3) **Individual Component Responsibilities.** Each component command will establish communications with the JSC and lateral organizations. Deficiencies in communications assets should be identified and resolved through the JFC.

(4) **Joint Movement Control Communications.** Communication to support LOC security operations must be coordinated with, and will often use, the joint movement control communications structure. This is especially true when LOC security operations are limited to internal convoy defense capabilities. See Chapter V, "Lines of Communications Security," for more information.

(5) **Inter-Service and Multinational and Contractor Communications System Challenges.** Often, tenant units, the program managers for contractors deploying with the force, or even MSF organizations will be operating with noncompatible communications equipment. The JSC and subordinate commanders responsible for planning and executing JSO must ensure that specific base, base cluster and LOC security communications measures are planned for and tested to ensure compatibility. If communications compatibility is identified as an issue, then proper "work-around" actions must be taken by the appropriate commander.

Further discussion of communications systems can be found in JP 6-0, Joint Communications System.

d. **Chemical, Biological, Radiological, and Nuclear Defense.** CBRN defensive operations are of primary importance to JSO and must be incorporated into all appropriate plans and procedures. Many potential threat forces have the capability to employ CBRN weapons to attack critical facilities and LOCs. All US forces in the operational area must be prepared to actively participate in the planning and execution of CBRN defensive operations.

(1) **Responsibilities of the JSC.** The JSC coordinates with component commanders and other appropriate commanders and staffs, ensuring that they incorporate appropriate CBRN defense planning, exercises, equipment, personnel decontamination measures, and preventive measures into overall security planning and operations. This responsibility includes due consideration for positioning of friendly CBRN defense assets to support current mission requirements and anticipated follow-on actions.

(2) **Responsibilities of Component Commanders.** Component commanders incorporate CBRN defense planning, exercises, equipment, personnel decontamination measures, and preventive measures into area and base or base cluster security plans. They also position friendly CBRN defense personnel and assets to support current mission requirements and facilitate future operations, IAW JFC directives and priorities.

(3) **Base and Base Cluster Commander.** Every base and base cluster commander integrates operational elements of CBRN defense designed to sense, shape, shield, and sustain against CBRN threats.

For further information on CBRN defensive operations see JP 3-11, Operations in Chemical, Biological, Radiological, and Nuclear (CBRN) Environments, *and Field Manual (FM) 3-11.34/Marine Corps Warfighting Publication (MCWP) 3.37.5/Navy Tactics,*

Techniques, and Procedures (NTTP) 3-11.23/Air Force Tactics, Techniques, and Procedures (Instruction) (AFTTP[I]) 3-2.33, Multi-Service Tactics, Techniques, and Procedures for Installation CBRN Defense.

e. **Air and Missile Defense.** Since most units operating on base and surface LOCs in the operational area have limited capability to engage and destroy incoming enemy air and missile threats; commanders must be aware of the capabilities and limitations of joint force defense counterair operations for their areas. The JSC's focus is protection for the JSAs. Dependent upon the size and scope of the JFC's mission, **the joint force may establish an integrated air defense system (IADS) to conduct defensive counterair operations**. The IADS is not a formal system in itself but the aggregate of component air defense systems operating in the operational area. The focal point of the IADS normally is the joint air operations center (JAOC). The JSC should establish effective liaison with the JFACC and AADC at the JAOC during development of the critical and defended lists to ensure that defensive counterair coverage is coordinated and maintained throughout the operational area to reduce or mitigate the effectiveness of the air and missile threat. That JSC liaison serves as the JSCs' eyes and ears as well as their representative on matters of Service capabilities and limitations. This integrated and coordinated air and missile defense planning must include detailed plans to disseminate timely air and missile warning and cueing information to components, forces, multinational partners, and civil authorities. Air and missile warning and cueing information for JSAs must be planned for and executed at the JSCC and down to each BDOC/BCOC. Special consideration must be given to the critical asset list and the defended asset list.

For more information on joint air and missile defense in general, see JP 3-01, Countering Air and Missile Threats, *Navy Warfare Publication (NWP) 3-01.01,* Fleet Air Defense, *MCWP 3-22,* Antiair Warfare, *Air Force Doctrine Document (AFDD) 2-1.1,* Counterair Operations, *and FM 44-100,* US Army Air and Missile Defense Operations.

f. **Threat Early Warning and Alert Notification System.** Threat early warning is essential to the protection of joint forces operating throughout the operational area and should be linked through the JSC and JSCC (if established) down through designated BCOCs and BDOCs. Alert notification systems are divided into two general categories.

(1) **Air Warning.** The air and missile defense warning system is a critical link in the operational area air early warning system. Early warning and identification of enemy air threats, enemy air- and surface-to-surface missiles, and airborne and air assault operations are provided by several types of forward collection methods, including forward-deployed reconnaissance units, air defense systems and the theater air ground system. A JFC's tactical warning requirements are supported by national and theater intelligence systems.

(2) **Surface, Subsurface, and Land Warning.** Information about potential surface, subsurface, and land threats are provided by various air, land, sea, and space intelligence, surveillance, and target acquisition systems. The CI element at the JIOC/JISE

will provide fused intelligence early warning of surface, subsurface or land threats to the bases and LOCs.

(3) The JSC coordinates with appropriate commanders and staffs to ensure that a reliable, responsive, and redundant air, land, and sea early warning system is established from the joint force level down to the base level throughout the operational area. The JSC will ensure that a standardized alert system is implemented throughout the JSA to ensure warning and uniform response to threats. Training should be conducted to ensure that all joint forces understand the correct responses to the various and sometimes confusing early warning alert notification systems.

(4) Land and maritime component commanders are responsible for ensuring that adequate early warning systems are established in their AO IAW JFC directives.

g. **Land Forces and Joint Security.** Joint security on the land includes bases, critical assets, lines of communications, and convoy security. Challenges include logistic facilities that may be located in heavily populated areas which are often linked by long and vulnerable surface lines of communications.

(1) In a JSA, multiple Service components may be using the same facilities within a base complex such as:

(a) Army intermediate staging bases, tactical assembly areas, or forward operating bases (FOBs).

(b) Army common-user water terminals.

(c) MAGTF support bases.

(d) Air Force air bases and airfields for APODs and close air support.

(e) Naval bases supporting and sustaining fleet operations.

(2) Joint Security and Protection

(a) Joint security operations requires fixing responsibility for protecting the joint force. A senior land commander will normally be designated with responsibility for joint security operations.

(b) When the Army is designated as the JFLCC, this responsibility is exercised through the designated protection cell. When designated as the JSC and responsible for the JSA, the Army headquarters protection cell (with augmented joint, interagency, and multinational personnel) provides the nucleus of the JSCC. The protection cell:

<u>1.</u> Integrates and synchronizes protection tasks and systems in the operations process.

<u>2.</u> Advises commanders on the priorities for protection and coordinates the implementation and sustainment of protective measures to protect assets according to the commander's priorities.

<u>3.</u> Provides input to the commander's plan by integrating the threat and hazard assessment to minimize vulnerability and provides vulnerability mitigation measures to help reduce risks.

(3) In support of the JFC's concept of operations, the JFLCC plans and conducts security operations to ensure protection of US and multinational critical assets and the support areas required for sustainment of land operations. The JFLCC will normally assign an Army maneuver enhancement brigade for security of defined geographic areas and to serve as its operational protection headquarters.

(a) Area security may be the predominant method of protecting support areas that are necessary to facilitate the positioning, employment, and protection of resources required to sustain, enable, and control tactical forces. Area security operations are often emphasized in noncontiguous AOs to compensate for the lack of protection integrity that large or distant, unoccupied areas often create. Area security operations are often an effective method of providing civil security and control during some stability operations. Forces engaged in area security operations can saturate an area or position on key terrain to provide protection through early warning, reconnaissance, or surveillance and guard against unexpected enemy attack with an active response.

(b) Base and base cluster defense are essential to joint land operations. Land forces may contribute to the protection of multiple FOBs within their respective support areas.

(c) The security and protection of lines of communications and supply routes are critical to joint land operations since most support traffic moves along these routes. The security of supply routes and LOCs (rail, pipeline, highway, and waterway) presents one of the greatest security problems in an operational area. Route security operations are defensive in nature and are terrain-oriented. A route security force may prevent an enemy force from impeding, harassing, or destroying traffic along a route or portions of a route by establishing a movement corridor. Units conduct synchronized operations (reconnaissance, security, mobility) within the movement corridor. A movement corridor may be established in a high-risk area to facilitate the movement of a single element, or it may be an enduring operation.

(4) US Army theater security organizations. The US Army has several organizations specifically designed and equipped to conduct security functions.

(a) Among the Army's modular support brigades, the maneuver enhancement brigade performs joint security and protection tasks. Maneuver enhancement brigades are designed to provide protection capabilities and other support to the joint force to include:

<u>1</u>. Engineer.

<u>2</u>. Military police.

<u>3</u>. CBRN.

<u>4</u>. Civil affairs

<u>5</u>. Air defense artillery.

<u>6</u>. Explosive ordnance disposal (EOD).

<u>7</u>. Tactical combat forces.

(b) Regional Support Groups. Army units specifically designed to serve as base headquarters and provide command and control, to include oversight of security for temporary bases.

(c) Rear operations centers (area) may provide augmentation for base command and control and security management for critical bases and facilities.

For more information, see FM 3-37, Protection.

h. **Maritime-Land Interface.** Bases established on a shoreline can present special advantages and challenges to those responsible for the functions inherent in the base's mission and for its defense. The advantages include the availability of the assets of more than one Service component for use by commanders in fulfilling their responsibilities. The special challenges may include the fact that facilities like ports and harbors are usually located in heavily populated areas.

(1) Command arrangements may be complicated by diverse purposes when multiple Service components use the same facilities. For example, the following installations may be in close geographical proximity.

(a) Army common-user water terminal.

(b) Support base for a MAGTF.

(c) Air Force base operating an APOD.

(d) Naval base supporting and sustaining fleet operations and/or maritime expeditionary security forces operations, naval advanced logistic support site, and naval forward logistic site.

(2) **Maritime Expeditionary Security Force (MESF)**

(a) In support of the JFC's concept of operations in time of war or contingency, MESFs plan and conduct operations to ensure strategic mobility and provide a safe haven for US and MNFs in coastal areas and for sustainment of land operations.

(b) **The JFC is responsible for maritime security.** This responsibility is exercised through the JFMCC, who will normally assign a commander to be in charge of maritime security forces for a defined geographic area. Maritime expeditionary security encompasses coastal sea control, harbor defense, and port security.

(c) The MESF commander may assign subarea operational commanders as needed for coastal sea control and harbor defense in order to conduct maritime expeditionary security operations such as intelligence gathering, reconnaissance and surveillance, interdiction, security and safety, and supporting operations.

(3) **Defense Planning.** Friendly naval forces are the primary defense against waterborne threats and should achieve maritime superiority in the waters adjacent to the base. However, even if overall superiority is achieved, small enemy units may seek to interfere with base operations from seaward approaches.

(a) **Amphibious Raids.** The enemy may attempt amphibious raids using watercraft and/or aircraft. Likely beaches, landing zones, and insertion areas should be guarded, obstacles should be placed, and the mobile reserve employed to counter such raids.

(b) **Sea Mining.** Enemy mining of the seaward approaches to the base can be conducted from surface vessels, by air, or clandestinely by submarines. Detection of such activity should be a priority effort for surveillance systems, patrol boats, and aircraft guarding the seaward approaches to the base.

(c) **Maritime Special Operations Forces.** Determined, specially trained, organized, and equipped individuals or units can infiltrate ports, harbors, and bases near shore by swimming, scuba diving, high-speed surface craft, indigenous small boats, or miniature submersibles. They can damage vessels, port facilities, and base resources. Security forces, both seaward and ashore, and their supporting surveillance systems must be prepared to locate and counter such threats.

(4) **Approaches to the Base.** Appropriate security and surveillance forces, backed up by capable MSFs, must be designated to cover every possible avenue of approach. These approaches include:

(a) Beaches.

(b) Concealed water approaches (fjords, bayous).

(c) Rivers.

(d) Drop zones and landing zones.

(e) Land approaches.

(f) Urban terrain and infrastructure (including underground water and sewage systems).

(g) Piers, docks, and waterfront facilities.

(5) **Navy and US Coast Guard (USCG) Organizations.** The MESF commander may assign a maritime expeditionary security squadron (MSRON) commander as the harbor defense commander (HDC). In concert with the MESF/MSRON commander, the HDC sets the boundaries for harbor defense. Defense of the harbor is the responsibility of the HDC, and inland defense is the responsibility of the appropriate area or component commander designated by the JFC. Close coordination on mission priorities must be accomplished for MESF units between the MESF commander and seaport/marine terminal commander to avoid conflicts. On a larger scale, under the direction of the MESF commander, the MSRON commander may have TACON of forces providing port security and harbor defense in more than one port and/or harbor. This may be particularly true along a coastline that has multiple ports in geographic proximity to each other. In this situation, the multiple ports may be designated a base cluster. The MSRON will, through the MESF commander, coordinate security operations with the appropriate area or functional commander. The MESF may possess some or all of the following capabilities.

(a) **Command and Control Division.** The C2 division is a mobile surveillance and detection unit that possesses surface search radar, thermal imaging and visual imaging cameras, and the mobile ashore support terminal to facilitate communications.

(b) **Boat Division.** A small craft unit consisting of eight 34-foot boats armed with crew served and personal weapons with the capability to detect and engage surface targets, conduct high-value asset escort, and provide harbor patrol.

(c) **Security Division.** Approximately 150 personnel armed with crew served and personal weapons designed for ashore protection of MESF. Capabilities include port security, entry control point protection, military aircraft protection, and garrison security.

(d) **Port Security Unit.** A USCG small craft unit consisting of six 25-foot boats armed with crew served and personal weapons; with the capability to detect and engage surface targets. This unit is integrated into the maritime component in wartime or as allowed by law. The unit also includes a waterfront security force to protect piers/wharves used in onload and offload operations. The mission of a PSU is to conduct port security and/or harbor JSO. PSU duties include patrolling harbors and anchorages, maritime interdiction, surveillance, and the enforcement of exclusionary zones.

(e) **Naval EOD Detachment.** This detachment provides ordnance handling and evaluation, special weapons and/or ammunition support, and mine detection and neutralization capabilities. This detachment also identifies mine and/or ordnance beaching areas for the port or harbor.

(f) **Mine Countermeasures (MCM) Elements.** These elements detect and destroy enemy mines in harbors, approaches, and sea-lanes, using MCM aircraft and vessels. Because of the small number of MCM forces, control of these assets is normally determined by the JFMCC.

(g) **Mobile Diving and Salvage Unit (MDSU).** The MDSU has the missions of underwater hull search and repair, channel clearance, vessel salvage, and pier and piling inspection and repair. The MSRON commander can request this unit's support of base defense efforts from the MESF commander when required.

(h) **Riverine Squadron (RIVRON).** The RIVRON consists of 12 heavily armed patrol craft capable of fire support, insertion of forces, or riverine control and/or denial.

(i) **Navy Expeditionary Logistics Support Group (NAVELSG).** NAVELSG, via the use of their Navy expeditionary logistics regiments, provides the capability and command and control of its Navy cargo handling battalions to conduct loading and discharging of military sealift shipping, either in-stream or pier side.

(6) Factors which should be considered when planning the defense of a base on a shoreline include the type and nature of the threat as well as protection for sea approach chokepoints, tides and currents, water clarity and depth, pier clearance, lighting, use of patrol boats, communications, rail and highway entrances security, air and missile defense measures, security for individual vessels, and ADC.

i. **Terrain Management and Infrastructure Development.** Effective terrain management and infrastructure development is critical to the success of JSO. The joint force must take advantage of security enhancement capabilities by using and enhancing available fixed and permanent installations, facilities, and fabrications. Infrastructure development focuses on facility security modification and damage repair in order to reduce the efforts that joint forces must make to heighten their base and LOC security posture. Additionally, use of HN manpower, medical support, equipment and materiel should be maximized.

(1) **Terrain Management Responsibilities**

(a) The JFC has overall responsibility for terrain management in the operational area and assigns specific terrain management responsibilities to subordinate commanders as appropriate.

(b) **The JSC coordinates terrain management within component capabilities.** The JSC's primary terrain management responsibility is to advise the commanders on the stationing of units and facilities in the JSA.

(c) **Component Commanders.** The JFLCC and JFMCC are responsible for terrain management within their AOs. They ensure that positioning of bases and stationing of units and facilities are made with due consideration for security.

(2) **Positioning Considerations**

(a) **Unit Positioning.** Factors affecting base and unit positioning include the implications of the current threat assessment, the suitability and survivability of available facilities, and the subordinate unit mission requirements. Component commanders and their staffs should use these factors and their own risk assessments to determine whether units should be dispersed or grouped together for mutual support.

(b) **Facility and Supply Positioning.** Factors affecting the positioning of facilities and supplies include the current threat assessment, the security implications, and the requirements of the units operating or using the facility and/or supplies, the impact of the facility or supplies on the joint force mission and/or concept of operation, LOCs, and accessibility. Considerations include those described in Figure III-3.

(3) **Infrastructure Development Responsibilities.** Joint forces deployed to developed areas should be able to capitalize on established infrastructure and the use of existing facilities. Joint forces deployed to less developed areas must rely more on construction of new but austere, initial, or temporary facilities IAW established base development criteria. HNS should be sought but will normally be less available than in developed areas.

(a) **GCC.** The GCC, in coordination with multinational partners as well as relevant USG/NGO entities and HN organizations, is responsible for identifying the wartime facility and construction requirements for US forces. During hostilities, the GCC specifies theater construction policy through the engineering support plan for each operation plan.

(b) **JSC.** The JSC coordinates to ensure that the JFC's construction policy in the JSA is implemented with due consideration to security concerns and requirements.

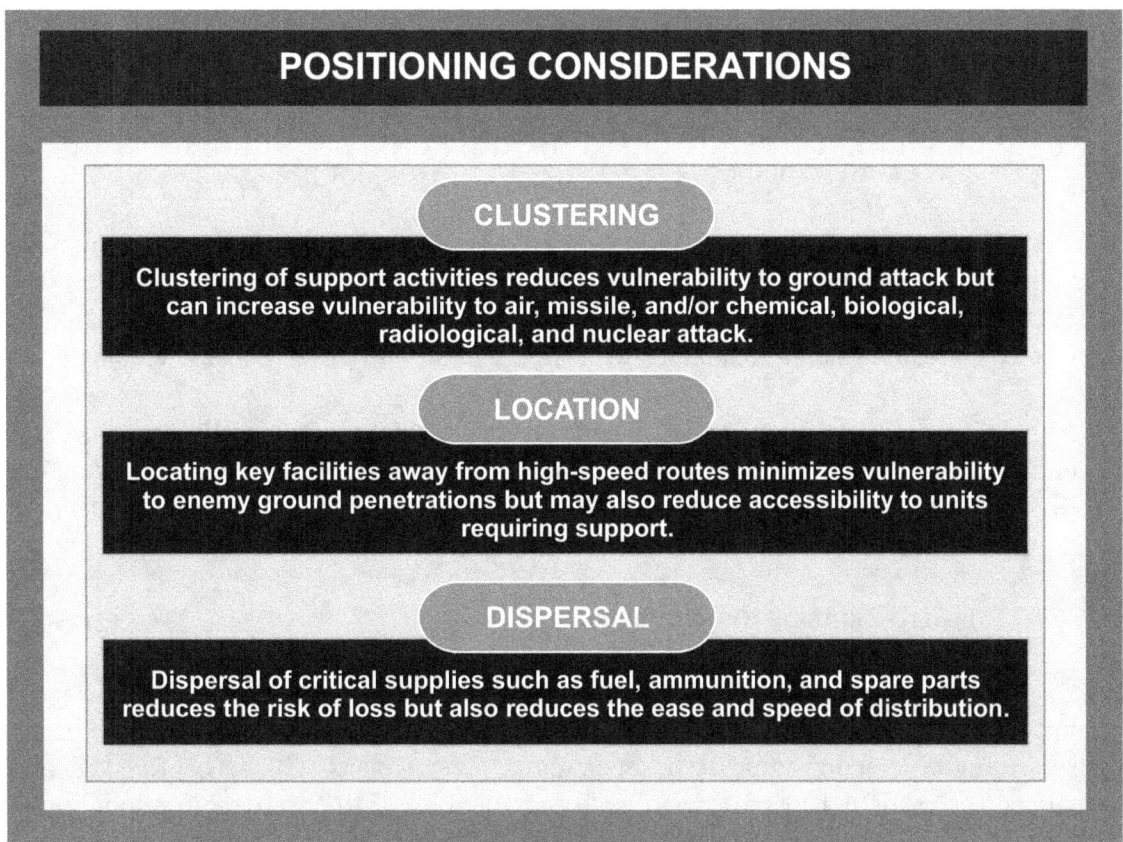

Figure III-3. Positioning Considerations

(c) **Commanders.** Commanders are responsible for implementing construction policy IAW JFC directives and guidelines. They plan and implement construction projects with due consideration to security concerns and requirements.

More information on base construction can be found in JP 3-34, Joint Engineer Operations.

j. **Area Damage Control.** ADC includes the measures taken before, during, and after hostile action or natural or man-made disasters to reduce the probability of damage and minimize its effects. Engineers perform most of these tasks. Other forces and assets contributing to ADC include combat support units, logistic units, tenant/transient units and HN units. **When an attack or natural disaster occurs, the objective is to continue regular operations by quickly restoring control, evacuating casualties, isolating danger areas, and replacing personnel and materiel losses.**

(1) **General.** Effective planning, establishment of specific responsibilities, and use of all available assets are necessary to conduct ADC and to ensure prevention, containment, and rapid restoration of operations.

(2) **Responsibilities**

(a) **JSC.** The JSC may advise appropriate commanders and staffs on ADC operations.

(b) **Area and Base Commanders.** Commanders are responsible for ensuring that ADC plans are developed, prioritized, coordinated, and executed.

(c) **Host Nation**

1. **Authority.** The HN, depending on applicable agreements, may have overall responsibility for ADC within its territorial boundaries. In these circumstances, US forces will retain responsibility for ADC within US base boundaries and be prepared to assist the HN within its unit capabilities with ADC operations outside US base boundaries.

2. **Assistance.** HNS agreements frequently address HN assistance for ADC operations. Commanders usually serve as single points of contact for coordinating ADC operations and, in that capacity, should ensure that HNS for ADC is planned, coordinated, prioritized, and executed IAW the JFC's priorities and concept of operation.

(3) **ADC Planning Requirements**

(a) **General.** ADC is executed at the lowest level. Base and base cluster security plans may have ADC annexes identifying responsibilities, priorities, requirements, and procedures for conducting ADC operations. These plans will be coordinated and integrated at the component and subordinate command levels to ensure rapid response and efficient use of limited ADC assets.

(b) **Specific Planning Responsibilities.** Base and base cluster ADC annexes should identify responsibilities and procedures required before, during, and after an incident. Plans should also include responsibilities for all units occupying the base or located in the base cluster that can make contributions to ADC. Examples include, but are not limited to, SF, engineers, ordnance, EOD, CBRN contamination avoidance and decontamination or reconnaissance, civil affairs, maintenance, medical support, communications systems, supply, and transportation.

k. **Integration of Joint Security and Logistic Operations.** Joint logistics integrates strategic, operational, and tactical level logistic operations. Maintaining movement control, keeping LOCs open, protecting key reception and transshipment points, protecting key logistic bases, and obtaining HNS are critically important JSO.

(1) **Responsibilities.** The JSC coordinates the overall security in the JSA and seeks joint security support of the joint force logistic concept of operations. **The JSC must coordinate with the JMC (if established) or other movement control agency on employment and joint security of all movements within the JSA.**

(2) **Other Considerations**

(a) **Medical Operations.** Enemy operations that interdict LOCs and disrupt sustainment activities could seriously impact the ability of medical support personnel to retrieve and evacuate wounded, sick, and injured personnel and provide timely medical care.

(b) The JFC should employ a joint movement control agency, center, or cell to conduct joint movement control planning, coordinate actions and resolve issues, especially with the HN, and act as the lead for joint movement control functions. The JSC should establish liaison with the JMC through the JSCC to monitor movements in the operational area.

For more information on joint movements and movement control see JP 4-09, Distribution Operations.

l. **Detainee Operations.** Planning for detainee operations is critical to the success of JSO. The JSC should establish planning mechanisms that ensure effective consideration of potential detainee-related issues and the development of plans and procedures to respond to these issues. Conducting appropriate planning will assist the JSC in mitigating possible detainee issues.

For additional information see JP 3-63, Detainee Operations.

5. **Other Major Planning Considerations**

The integration of all US military capabilities, often in conjunction with forces from other nations, other US agencies, NGOs, HN civil authorities, and HN security forces and authorized civilians accompanying the joint force, requires effective and efficient JSO planning. **The JSC coordinates the overall security of bases and LOCs through the integration and synchronization of HNS, multinational operations, civil-military operations (CMO), and interagency coordination.** The goal is to maximize the effectiveness of the base and LOC security forces through the proper employment of all security assets.

a. **Host-Nation Support**

(1) The effective use of HNS enhances the capability of US forces to achieve success during any military operation. Many HNs can provide valuable support for conducting security operations. **The JSC and appropriate subordinate commanders must consider HN capabilities when planning and conducting security operations.** HN personnel and organizations can frequently perform many functions as well as, or better than, US personnel or units because of their familiarity with language, local customs, terrain, transportation and communications networks, facilities, and equipment. The scope of HNS is limited by the availability of resources, equipment interoperability, the capability of the HN, and the ability of the United States and the HN to reach agreements concerning their use.

CONVOY OPERATIONS TRAINING

Due to the high-threat nature of the lines of communications in Operation IRAQI FREEDOM, the Army established a major in-theater tactical convoy operations training program for all deploying Army units. In addition to Army units, selected other Service units and contractor personnel went through this major live-fire training as part of their in-theater pre-employment preparation. This convoy training included both classroom and hands-on training that included close-quarters marksmanship, shooting from moving vehicles, recovery of damaged vehicles while under fire, and other convoy tactic-related actions.

SOURCE: *Stars and Stripes*, **March 2004**

(2) **Responsibilities**

(a) **JSC.** The JSC, coordinating with appropriate commanders and the HN lead staff (if designated), ensures that HN security assets are used to enhance the overall security of the military forces and support the JFC's current and future concept of operations.

(b) **Component Commanders.** Component commanders are responsible for the use and employment of HNS IAW JFC directions and guidelines. When HNS security assets are available, component commanders' responsibilities include ensuring that the following applies.

1. HN security assets dedicated to US forces are used and positioned to help defend bases, LOCs and facilities and can support the JFC's current and future concept of operations.

2. US base and base cluster defense plans are coordinated with and complement HN overall security plans.

3. Appropriate HN commands are advised of US forces' priorities for security.

(3) **Considerations. HNS is normally based on agreements that commit the HN to provide specific support in prescribed conditions.** Agreements are made at various levels, including national, theater, subordinate joint force command, functional component command (e.g., JFLCC), Service component command, and the local unit. In general, HNS is highly situational and heavily dependent on both the operational capabilities of the HN and its support for US policies.

(a) **Command and Control.** US and HN commanders command their respective units and normally work ICW each other. In some instances, forces from one command may be placed under TACON of the other. The degree of coordination between

---

US forces and HNS activities depends on the type of HNS involved, the location, tactical situation, the political environment, and existing agreements. The USG coordinates its control of HN resources through local officials or HN territorial commands and defines control with treaties or HNS agreements. When an established US military structure is absent, the SDO assigned to the US embassy country team will normally be the point of contact for US forces' coordination of HNS requirements.

(b) **Training.** US personnel at all levels should receive training in dealing with HN personnel, both on and off duty. Orientation should include HN government regulations, business practices, social customs, military procedures, religious customs, and language familiarity. Frequent training in security awareness, base security plans, LOC security, and safety should be provided to those HN units charged with support of the defense effort.

(c) **HN Security Support.** Many HNs can and do provide extensive support for security-related activities. Specific types of HN security support are depicted in Figure III-4 and are described below.

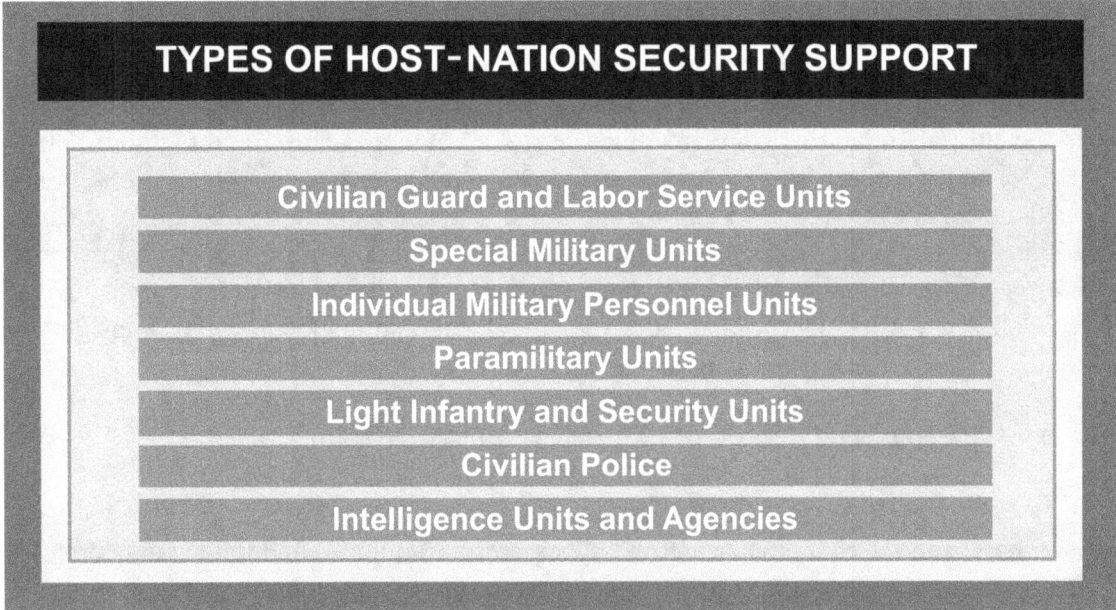

Figure III-4. Types of Host-Nation Security Support

1. **Civilian Guard and Labor Service Units.** These units are usually in place during peacetime or developed after the commencement of hostilities. The use of civilian guards after hostilities commence will be on a case-by-case basis based on circumstances in the operational area and as directed by the GCC.

2. **Special Military Units.** These units are designed during peacetime to perform specific wartime missions, such as guarding enemy prisoners of war and detainees and securing valuable facilities, materiel, or ammunition. Included in this group are HN

MP units, which provide support but are not necessarily assigned or totally dedicated to US forces.

3. **Individual Military Personnel Units.** These personnel may be used as fillers for selected HN units, which provide individual HN personnel in order to support US forces, such as the Korean augmentation to the US Army in Korea.

4. **Paramilitary Units.** Some nations' police are paramilitary in nature, such as Belgium's Gendarmerie, and function in both civilian and military roles. They have significantly more utility for HNS in a hostile environment than normal civilian police.

5. **Light Infantry and Security Units.** Most HN countries use these types of units as their primary security forces. They are frequently given both area and point security missions.

6. **Civilian Police.** These organizations frequently assist US MP and SF forces during peacetime, but have significantly less capability during wartime.

7. **Intelligence Units and Agencies.** HNS intelligence organizations may be employed to assist in providing essential elements of information to the JFC's base and LOC security plan. Base commanders must ensure that HN intelligence elements link with the JFC and other joint force intelligence staffs. HN agencies are normally excellent HUMINT and CI sources. HN organizations can provide tactical intelligence on enemy ground, naval, and air forces, CI on foreign intelligence and security service threat, terrorist intentions and collection capabilities, and interrogation and debriefing reports from enemy prisoners of war (EPWs), other detainees, refugees, returnees, and enemy sympathizers. HN intelligence personnel would add valuable local and national cultural insight to currently held intelligence assessments and data.

For more information on HNS see JP 3-57, Civil-Military Operations.

(d) **HNS in CBRN Environment.** When required, HN military, paramilitary, and selected civilians providing support are equipped and trained to operate in a CBRN environment. Training and equipping are normally national responsibilities. In the event of a CBRN attack or CBRN environment, many types of HNS may be needed. The need of HNS may be due to limited CBRN defense supplies and/or units. Some of the types of HNS that can be requested are decontaminates, water, water transportation assets, CBRN detection devices, engineer digging equipment or units, and decontamination equipment or units.

For further information on CBRN defensive measures see JP 3-11, Operations in Chemical, Biological, Radiological, and Nuclear (CBRN) Environments.

b. **Multinational Operations**

(1) **Integrating Multinational Forces into JSO.** The JFC establishes coordination with MNF and HN commands IAW existing agreements at all appropriate levels within the joint force. In some instances or contingencies, the JFC will have access to the US ambassador and his country team for help in the coordination process. Intelligence and operations liaison within and between bases, base clusters and higher headquarters is essential in developing security plans and executing defensive operations. Early and continuous liaison with MNF and HN and allied organizations, and with established MSFs, must be conducted to ensure effective and coordinated actions when required.

(2) **Command and Control of US Forces in Multinational Operations.** The President of the United States always retains direct command authority over US forces. This includes the authority and responsibility for effectively using available resources and for planning, organizing, directing, coordinating, controlling, and protecting military forces for the accomplishment of assigned missions. It is sometimes prudent or advantageous, however, to place appropriate US forces under the operational control (OPCON) or TACON of a foreign commander to achieve specified joint security related military objectives. In making the determination to place US forces under the OPCON or TACON of non-US commanders, the US President must carefully consider such factors as the mission, size of the proposed US force, risks involved, anticipated duration, and ROE.

(3) **Host Nation and MNF.** Host nation and MNF governments, represented by their military forces and law enforcement agencies, generally will have responsibility for many base and LOC security functions. The JFC will coordinate US MNF and HNS requirements with MNF and HN commands.

See JP 3-16, Multinational Operations, *for more information on multinational operations.*

c. **Civil-Military Operations.** CMO assist the JSC in establishing and maintaining positive relationships between assigned forces, civil authorities, and the population. **CMO are critically important to ensure civil authority and popular understanding of, as well as compliance with, military security measures.** They enhance support for US forces and alleviate conditions that may result in local interference with military operations. Likewise, CMO are key in ensuring that JSO impacts on local civilian populace are also considered and lessened if feasible. Consideration of the impact JSO can have on the civil populace can be very important, especially in long-term stability operations. The JSC coordinates with the component commanders to ensure that they incorporate CMO procedures into all JSO. The proper employment of CMO assets can greatly enhance the JSC's ability to integrate US, multinational, and HN security forces, as well as HN government agencies and NGOs. Component commanders are responsible for CMO within their AO IAW the JFC's directives. CMO personnel and forces can assist in conducting joint and multinational security operations by providing assessments on local civilian capabilities and vulnerabilities in such areas as public facilities, transportation, and supplies. They can provide interface and coordination directly with designated civil agencies and authorities to facilitate or develop the objectives shown in Figure III-5.

OBJECTIVES OF CIVIL-MILITARY OPERATIONS IN JOINT SECURITY OPERATIONS

- Enhance base and lines of communications security measures

- Reduce civil interference with joint security operations

- Reduce impact of joint security operations on the civilian population

- Assist in the integration of civil security and defense assets

- Assist in the coordination of relief efforts by governmental and intergovernmental agencies

- Enhance civil information activities, in conjunction with psychological operations programs, to dispel rumor and disinformation generated by hostile elements

Figure III-5. Objectives of Civil-Military Operations in Joint Security Operations

Additional information on CMO can be found in JP 3-57, Civil-Military Operations.

d. **Interagency, Intergovernmental Organization, and Nongovernmental Organization Coordination**

> *"Joint force commanders frequently state that interagency coordination is one of their biggest challenges. To that end, commanders must understand the principles of interagency coordination and bring them to bear during joint and multinational operations."*
>
> **General John M. Shalikashvili, US Army**
> **Chairman of the Joint Chiefs of Staff**
> **October 1996**

(1) Interagency coordination is the coordination that occurs between agencies of the USG, including the DOD, for the purpose of accomplishing an objective. Similarly, in the context of DOD involvement, IGO and NGO coordination refer to coordination between elements of DOD and IGOs or NGOs to achieve an objective. The integration of US political and military objectives and the subsequent translation of these objectives into demonstrable action have always been essential to success at all levels of joint operation.

(2) The JSC, with the assistance of joint force CMO assets and reach back to the geographic combatant command joint interagency coordination group, integrates JSO with the activities of other agencies of the USG, NGOs, IGOs, regional organizations, and the operations of HN forces and activities of various HN agencies conducting security operations in the GCC's AOR and/or the JOA. By understanding the interagency coordination process, the JSC will be better able to appreciate how the skills and resources

of the various USG agencies interact with NGOs, IGOs, and regional organizations to assist in the overall security posture of the joint force.

(3) **NGOs.** Where long-term problems precede a deepening crisis, NGOs are frequently on scene before the US military and are often willing to operate in high-risk areas. They will most likely remain long after military forces have departed. Because of their capability to respond quickly and effectively to crises, they can lessen the civil-military resources that a JFC would otherwise have to devote to a joint operation. NGOs may range in size and experience from those with multimillion dollar budgets and decades of global experience in developmental and humanitarian relief to newly created small organizations dedicated to a particular emergency or disaster. The US President, through the GCC, may determine that it is in the national interest to task US military forces to provide security for NGOs, which in most instances is mutually beneficial since military assistance to NGOs has often proven to be the critical difference that enabled the success of joint operations.

For further information on interagency, IGO, and NGO coordination see JP 3-08, Interorganizational Coordination During Joint Operations.

e. **DOD Civilian Work Force and DOD Contractor Employees**

(1) **General.** US forces seldom deploy for contingency operations without a significant number of supporting DOD civilians and contractor personnel. Civilians accompanying the force provide support to military forces across the range of military operations. Their contributions to the force are critical to the success of today's joint operations. **The management, control, and security of the DOD civilian work force and contingency contractor personnel are a unique and significant challenge for the JFC, subordinate JFC and Service component commands.**

(2) **DOD Civilian Workforce.** The DOD civilian work force is defined as US citizens or foreign nationals hired directly or indirectly to work for the DOD, paid from appropriated or nonappropriated funds under permanent or temporary appointment. This includes employees filling full-time, part-time, intermittent, or on-call positions. The DOD civilian work force should be prepared to respond rapidly, efficiently, and effectively to meet mission requirements for all contingencies and emergencies.

(a) Plans, programs, contingency and emergency manpower requirements, and an appropriate state of readiness, including organization infrastructure, should be developed as an integral part of the continuing activities of each DOD component.

(b) As an integral part of the total force, **the deployed DOD civilian work force will follow the JFC's force protection and other joint security policies and operational direction when employed in or deployed in support of military operations**. They should be processed and supported in the same manner as military personnel of their employing component, as permissible by law and/or existing SOFAs with foreign nations.

(c) **Responsibilities**

1. The JFC and DOD components should develop, maintain, and exercise civilian contingency and emergency plans and procedures to implement DOD planning guidance and policy to prepare the civilian work force for employment and deployment to support all contingencies and emergencies rapidly, efficiently, and effectively. The GCC will establish civilian work force accountability procedures to include names, numbers, locations, and status of deployed individuals. The GCC should also issue theater specific admission requirements for civilians and includes summaries of civilian work force status to their situational reports and comply with all requirements of Department of Defense Directive (DODD) 1400.31, *DOD Civilian Work Force Contingency and Emergency Planning and Execution,* with regard to the civilian work force.

2. The JSC should monitor DOD component and GCC compliance with all civilian work force contingency and emergency plans and procedures to ensure the proper level of security is accorded to all of the civilian work force.

(3) Contingency contractor personnel will provide support to US military forces across the full range of military operations. They include all DOD contract personnel and their subcontractor personnel, including US citizens, third country nationals (TCNs) and local national personnel who are hired by and provide support to US military forces in contingency operations under such contracts. **DOD contingency contractor personnel are separate and distinct from contractor employees working for the Department of State or other government agencies (OGAs), even when their contracts are administered by a US military contracting agency.** The JFC may have limited responsibility for the security of OGA personnel to include OGA contractors.

(a) DOD contingency contractor personnel include **system support, external support, and theater support** personnel. System support contractors and many external support contractor personnel deploy with the force and are referred to as contractors authorized to accompany the force (CAAF). CAAF personnel often have a habitual relation with, reside with, and provide direct support to US military units. **CAAF personnel for the most part are treated similar to DOD civilians in relation to joint security, AT, and FP programs.** They are, in accordance with their contract, required to abide by JFC and component AT and FP as well as other joint security related directives and policies.

(b) Non-CAAF personnel include theater support and some external support contractors, local nationals, and TCNs. These locally hired personnel often reside off base and will, in general, be provided incidental security support when they are working on a military base or in close proximity to US forces. Use of local national or TCN or theater support contractor employees must be carefully considered from the base security perspective. **In some operational situations, the use of local national and some TCN personnel can carry significant security, and even medical, risks.** Figure III-6 provides basic points of consideration related to the use of local national and TCN contract employees to support base operations.

BASE SECURITY CONSIDERATIONS: USE OF NON-US CONTRACTOR PERSONNEL

➤ Will these contractor personnel reside on base or live off base?

➤ If they live off base, what base access control measures are required?

➤ How will access be controlled to specific areas within the base?

➤ Is there a vetting and badging process in place? If so, who will enforce it and how?

➤ Will these contractor personnel be physically screened and/or searched in order to enter the base?

➤ Will armed escorts be required? If so, who will do this? How will this requirement be resourced?

Figure III-6. Base Security Considerations: Use of Non-US Contractor Personnel

(c) **Responsibilities.** CCDRs, subordinate JFCs, Service components and DOD agencies shall:

1. Ensure operational specific contractor policies and requirements are identified in appropriate plans and orders. This integrated planning includes the Service components and DOD agencies coordinating any proposed contractor support arrangements that may impact the operation plan or operation order (OPORD).

2. Ensure the contract clearly and accurately specifies the terms and conditions under which the contractor is to perform, describes the specific support relationship between the contractor and the DOD, and contains standardized clauses to ensure efficient deployment/redeployment, management, protection, authorized levels of health service and other support, and sustainment.

3. Develop a security plan for protection of contingency contractor personnel in locations where there is not sufficient protection. In appropriate cases, the GCC may provide security through military means, commensurate with the level of security provided DOD civilians.

4. Monitor component compliance with contractor personnel contingency and emergency plans and procedures to ensure the proper level of security is accorded.

(d) **Security Related Considerations for Contractors**

<u>1</u>. Area commanders, base commanders and supported unit commanders are responsible for providing individual AT and FP support, and may be responsible for providing security to contractor personnel. To properly accomplish this task, area commanders must have oversight of all supporting contingency contractor personnel in their AO.

<u>2</u>. Contractors must ensure that their employees follow all security and individual FP requirements and oversight organization policies stated in the contract. Contractors are expected to take passive FP measures for the safety and security. Also, contractors should mandate measures for self-defense such as conducting driving classes, issuing cell phones, and establishing procedures for reporting suspicious incidents.

<u>3</u>. Contingency contractor personnel may be armed for self-defense pursuant to DOD policy and subject to US HN law and international law, and relevant SOFAs and international agreements. All requests for permission to arm contingency contractor personnel must be reviewed by the appropriate GCC's staff judge advocate (SJA).

For more information, see Department of Defense Instruction (DODI) 3020.41, Contractor Personnel Authorized to Accompany the US Armed Forces.

<u>4</u>. Security contractors should not be used to protect US or coalition military forces, facilities and supply routes in areas where major combat operations are on-going or imminent, except as specifically authorized by the GCC. Security contractors may be employed to protect selected military assets in areas where major combat in not imminent or ongoing if consistent with applicable US, HN, and international law, and relevant SOFAs or other international agreements.

<u>5</u>. The use of force by contingency contractor personnel is strictly limited by laws and not protected by SOFA provisions. The combatant command SJA must ensure that any use of contracted security forces to protect US military forces, facilities and supplies is done IAW applicable internal, US and local law.

For more information, see DODI 3020.41, Contractor Personnel Authorized to Accompany the US Armed Forces.

<u>6</u>. CAAF and selected other contingency contractor personnel should, as a minimum, receive information on local and security procedures, be issued CBRN and other protection equipment (along with the requisite training), and travel/movement security support. Such training and equipment should be designated in the contract and be given before deployment at the designated deployment center. Operational specific FP and general security training required by non-CAAF will be determined and executed by the JFC and applicable component commanders and/or DOD agency.

<u>7</u>. The issue of contractor security forces C2, ROE/RUF, and their role should be addressed by the GCC in each individual theater, the terms of the contract, and

the appropriate service regulations. Additional, overarching guidance and information can be found in JP 4-10, *Operational Contract Support.*

   f. **Laws, Agreements, and Other Legal Constraints**

      (1) Commanders at all levels are to have access to professional legal advice with regard to the legal aspects of the use of force in security operations. International law, US law and HN law are all relevant. Together, they regulate the status and activities of US forces across the range of military operations. This section provides a very basic summary of principal legal instruments that may impact on joint security.

      (2) **Responsibilities**

         (a) The **GCC** coordinates with appropriate commanders and staffs to ensure the law of armed conflict, established ROE, US law, international agreements, HN laws and other legal issues are considered and adhered to in conducting JSO.

         (b) **Component and Base Commanders.** Component and base commanders ensure that JFC ROE is disseminated and shared to all members of the joint force operating in or passing through their AO or base. They ensure that laws, regulations, and procedures regarding treatment of detainees are disseminated and shared to all appropriate US forces and that adequate liaison is established with HN authorities in order to coordinate these actions when required. They ensure that legal representatives are available to assist US forces and to coordinate with friendly HN authorities on such matters as HN supply for US forces, acquisition of HN and enemy materiel, responsibility for the handling of EPWs or other detainees, division of police authority between HN and US forces, and responsibility for ADC.

         (c) In certain contingency operations, the JFC may have no HNS or operate in a noncooperative HN and will have full responsibility for all joint security functions. Therefore, the JFC must plan for and be prepared to execute all JSA functions with or without HNS.

      (3) **Rules of Engagement.** ROE are directives issued by competent military authority that delineate the circumstances and limitations under which US forces will initiate and/or continue combat engagement with other forces encountered. The GCC establishes ROE for the AOR IAW guidance from the President and SecDef. Requests to modify ROE can be made by a subordinate JFC or local commander. All ROE, to include security operations related ROE, must conform to the law of war, but the formulation process also takes into account operational, political, and diplomatic factors such as HN laws concerning defense of others, self defense, and protection of military facilities. As a result, ROE may restrict or prohibit some uses of force that the law of armed conflict would allow. (NOTE: ROE may change at national boundaries.)

      (4) **US Law.** US forces, regardless of location, follow US law as expressed in statutes, executive orders, DOD directives and instructions, Service regulations, and

geographic combatant and component command directives, OPORDs and regulations promulgated under the law as well as international agreements concluded pursuant to US law. Civilian employees and contractors overseas accompanying the Armed Forces of the United States may be prosecuted for violations of US law under either Article 2 of the Uniform Code of Military Justice (during time of declared war or contingency operation), or under the Military Extra-territorial Jurisdiction Act if certain requirements are met. Joint force security directives issued by the GCC and by the component commanders are subject to applicable SOFAs or similar agreements. For specific publications containing applicable US laws and SOFAs contact the US embassy SDO or GCC's legal adviser. Some SOFAs and similar agreements are classified.

(5) **International Agreements.** The Armed Forces of the United States are committed to conducting joint operations according to the applicable provisions of the law of armed conflict, including those of The Hague and Geneva Conventions. International agreements are the primary source of rules of international law applicable to US, multinational, and HN forces. The most comprehensive are SOFAs; however, these may be modified or become inapplicable in time of armed conflict. They prescribe most of the reciprocal rights, powers, duties, privileges, and immunities of the US forces to include DOD civilians and contractor personnel stationed abroad and of the governments of the host and allied/coalition nations and their respective armed forces. Other important types of international agreements concern security assistance and HN support agreements. For specific information on HN support agreements (e.g., acquisition and cross-servicing agreements) and international agreements (e.g., defense cooperation agreements) contact the US embassy military SDO or GCC's legal advisor.

(6) **HN Laws.** HN laws apply to individual members of the US forces in the HN, unless specifically modified or made not applicable to US forces by the terms of an international agreement. HN laws have broad as well as finite implications on the conduct of all functions related to JSO. Obligations that the law of war imposes on the US can take precedence over HN laws. US advisers, commanders, staff officers, DOD civilians, and Service members must understand critical HN laws and the provisions of DOD and Service policies concerning HNS.

(7) **Detainee Operations.** Commanders at all levels must plan for and anticipate the capture of detainees. Commanders must take the appropriate measures to ensure fair and equitable treatment is afforded to all detainees.

See JP 3-63, Detainee Operations, *for additional information.*

CHAPTER IV
SECURITY OF BASES AND BASE CLUSTERS

"Rear guards are the safety of armies and often they carry victory with them."

Frederick the Great
Instructions to his Generals
1747

1. Introduction

The JFC, with or without a formally designated JSC, assigns and controls forces that are responsible to execute base and base cluster security operations. **Key to establishing successful base security is to ensure there is a proactive base security posture.** Security forces must be trained, organized and equipped to properly execute base and base cluster security against Level I and II threats, and if required, be prepared to engage Level III threats. This chapter sets forth the considerations, as well as guidance for base and base cluster security operations. This chapter also provides discussion on defensive considerations against Level III threats.

2. Tenets for Joint Security Operations

In order to be successful, certain fundamental tenets are essential for successful joint security operations. These include knowledge of the enemy, unity of command, economy of force and responsiveness. While of equal importance, paramount in the conduct of joint security operations is the availability of well trained forces to provide a timely and often immediate response to threats. These tenets are discussed below in Figure IV-1.

3. Base and Base Cluster Operations Overview

The JSC, ICW the base and base cluster commanders, coordinates the forces of the various Service or functional components to best capitalize on their combined capabilities while minimizing the vulnerabilities of each.

a. **Base.** A base is a locality from which operations are projected or supported. **At the base level, the component in command of the base has overall responsibility for the security of everything within the base boundary.** Tenant units normally secure their own facilities within the base, but selected forces will be made available by tenant units and the base commander will exercise TACON over those forces for the purpose of base defense. This will be commensurate with their capabilities and the local threat.

b. **Base Cluster.** A base cluster is a collection of bases, geographically grouped for mutual protection and ease of C2. The base cluster commander will be appointed by the JFC or his designated representative and may be the next higher tactical C2 headquarters of the base, the senior base commander, or another designated base commander, depending on the situation. There is no fixed number of bases in a base cluster, but typically a base

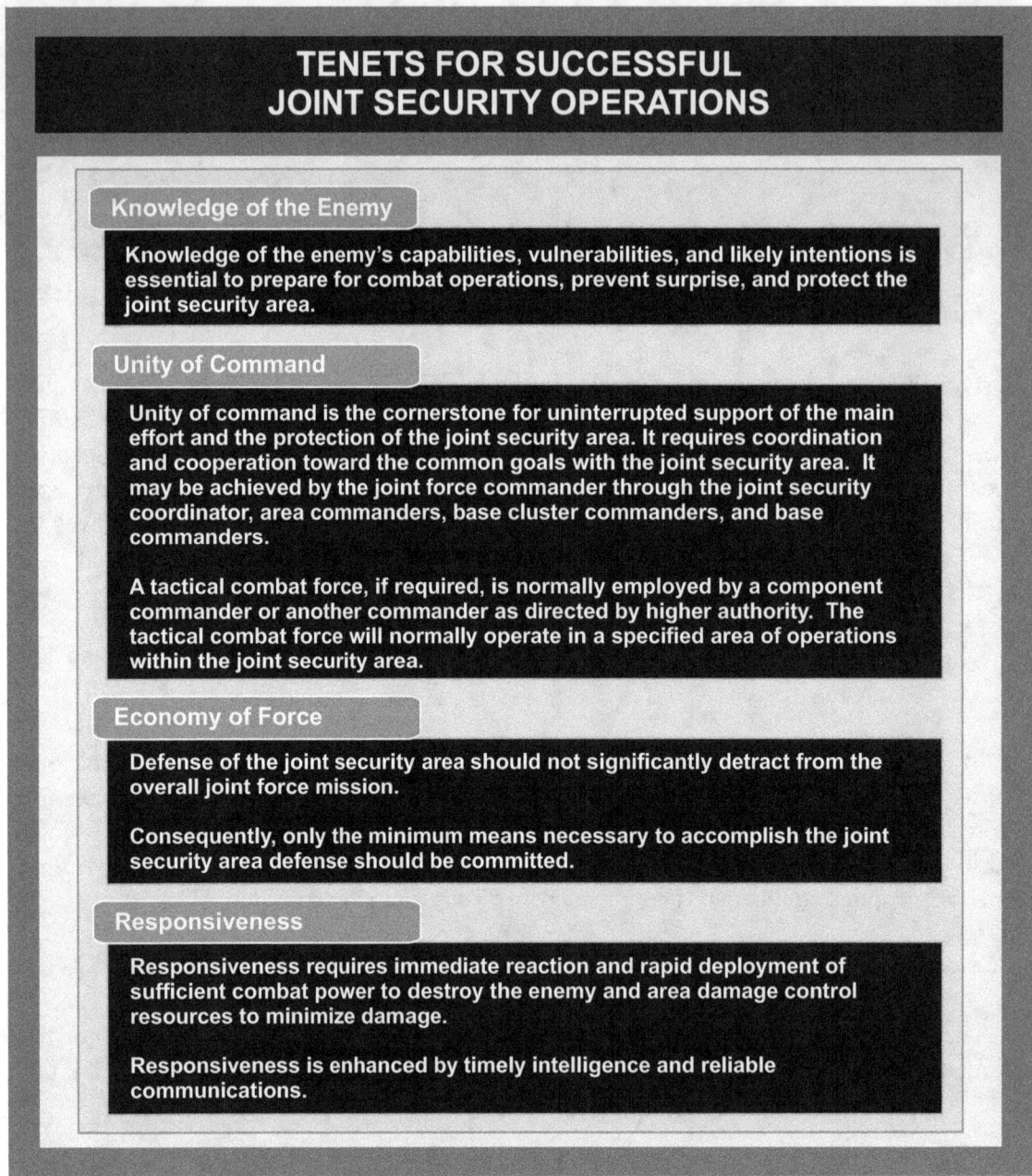

TENETS FOR SUCCESSFUL JOINT SECURITY OPERATIONS

Knowledge of the Enemy

Knowledge of the enemy's capabilities, vulnerabilities, and likely intentions is essential to prepare for combat operations, prevent surprise, and protect the joint security area.

Unity of Command

Unity of command is the cornerstone for uninterrupted support of the main effort and the protection of the joint security area. It requires coordination and cooperation toward the common goals with the joint security area. It may be achieved by the joint force commander through the joint security coordinator, area commanders, base cluster commanders, and base commanders.

A tactical combat force, if required, is normally employed by a component commander or another commander as directed by higher authority. The tactical combat force will normally operate in a specified area of operations within the joint security area.

Economy of Force

Defense of the joint security area should not significantly detract from the overall joint force mission.

Consequently, only the minimum means necessary to accomplish the joint security area defense should be committed.

Responsiveness

Responsiveness requires immediate reaction and rapid deployment of sufficient combat power to destroy the enemy and area damage control resources to minimize damage.

Responsiveness is enhanced by timely intelligence and reliable communications.

Figure IV-1. Tenets for Successful Joint Security Operations

cluster contains two to seven bases. **The JFC, normally through the JSC, designates each base cluster.**

c. **Base Security Forces.** A base security force **is a security element established to provide local security to a base**. It normally consists of the combined dedicated and on-call forces assigned or attached and those forces from tenant units attached with specification of TACON for base defense or security operations. It may also include a MSF consisting of MP, SF, or combat arms units. The mission of the base security force is to counter Level I and II threats. **The base commander normally appoints a base security force commander to execute FP, security, and defense functions within the base**

boundary. This individual will plan and execute all base security IAW the base commander's guidance. The base commander tasks units located within the base to provide personnel, equipment, and materiel to form or augment the base security force.

d. **Command and Control Considerations. The area commander, normally a combat arms land force commander, is responsible to provide security support to all bases and base clusters (if designated) within the command's AO. This responsibility will often include bases that are commanded by organizations not part of the area commander's forces. The base cluster commander has direct responsibility for area security within the assigned cluster.** In cases where the isolated base commander has no dedicated land combat arms forces, the base commander, ICW the JSC, should normally form a MSF capable of conducting area security operations needed to protect the base. This may entail operations outside the base boundary. In all cases, command arrangements and joint security operation directives, orders and policies must be clearly established for all anticipated situations. The following diagrams in Figure IV-2 illustrate a number of considerations for establishing the base boundary. When HN, urban terrain, and other factors constrain the size of the base boundary, the base commander must coordinate/integrate proactive security operations with the area commander or HN to counter the threat of standoff attacks or assume the risk.

e. **Work Priorities.** Base and base cluster commanders must set priorities for tasks involved in base security. Work may occur on several concurrent tasks. Figure IV-3 reflects some key base security work priorities.

4. Security in Level I and Level II Threat Environments

a. **General.** Base and base cluster commanders develop security plans in order to organize base security operations. **Successful security depends on an integrated and aggressive plan consisting of on-call base security**, dedicated SF, base or base cluster MSFs, and ADC response services (medical, fire fighting, and engineer). Actions against enemy threats and other potential emergencies to include natural disasters and accidents must be planned for and adjustments to base or base cluster security plans made. Drawing from the units available, commanders organize SF within their bases and base clusters. The base commander integrates the base security plans with those of its base cluster.

(1) Base SF should have a high degree of direct-fire lethality to cope with potential threats. This may include a mixture of small arms, automatic weapons, and antitank systems. The MSF should also have access to supporting indirect fires, a high degree of tactical mobility and a reasonable span of C2. A base security force should be capable of:

(a) Conducting reconnaissance patrols for detecting and reporting the location, strength, and capabilities of enemy forces located near the base and both landward and seaward if base is at a SPOD or seaport.

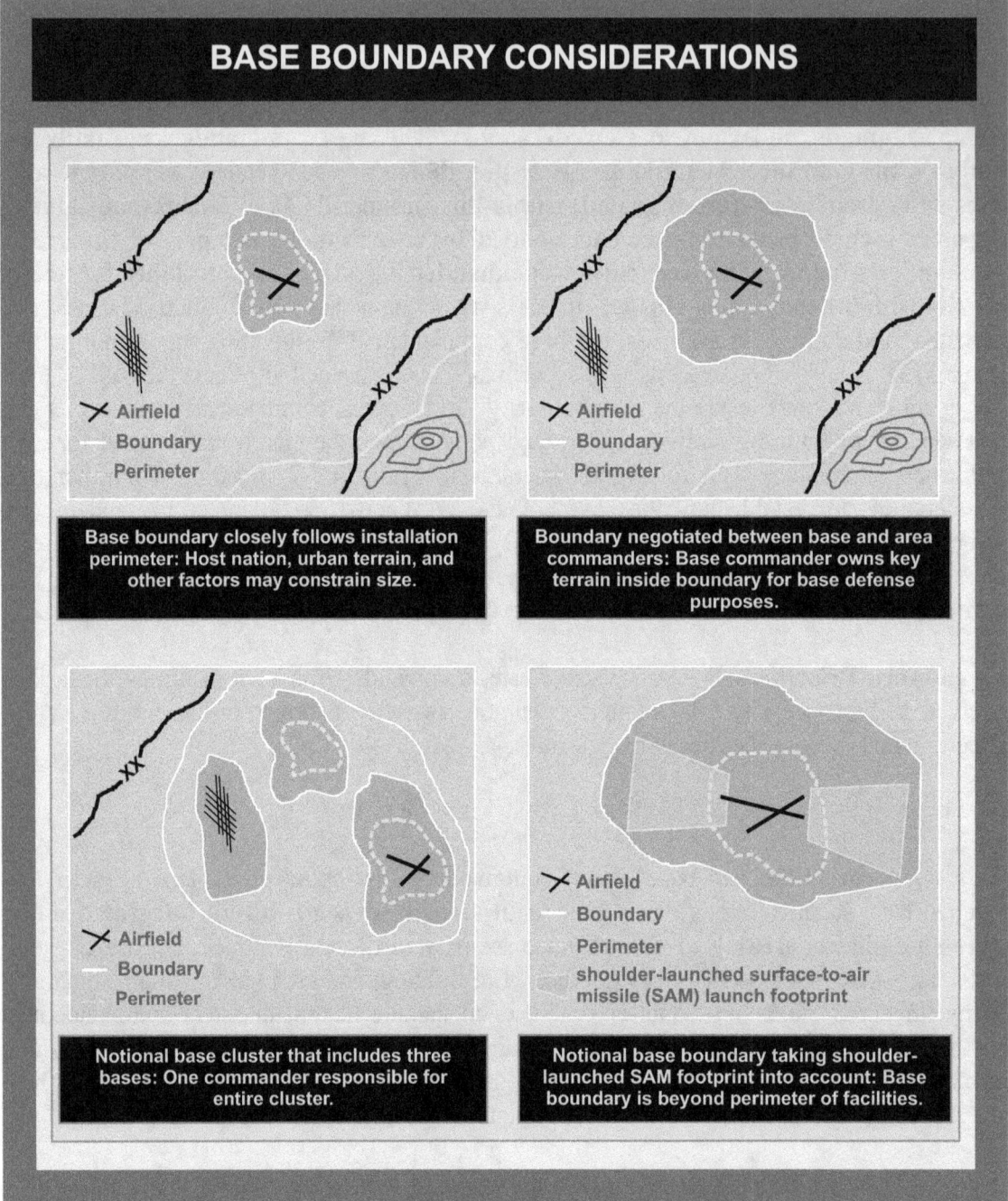

Figure IV-2. Base Boundary Considerations

(b) Developing fighting positions within the base from which enemy advances can be stopped or destroyed.

(c) Developing and conducting a patrol plan to deny the enemy key terrain from which to conduct standoff attacks.

(d) Fusing tactical intelligence sources to execute/coordinate proactive combat operations.

BASE SECURITY WORK PRIORITIES

- Preparation of a base security plan

- Establishment of appropriate perimeter standoff based on threat and host nation situation

- Establishment of vehicle and personnel entry points and search areas

- Establishment of access control processes, badges, and local national labor and visitor control procedures

- Construction of personnel survivability shelters in vicinity of work centers, living areas, and recreation facilities

- Establishment of attack warning systems (including alarms, codes, actions and means of population education)

- Integration of host nation or coalition forces as required

- Establishment of mass casualty procedures and capabilities

- Development of joint coordinated fire plan

- Conduct rehearsals

- Establishment/coordination of active patrols and tactical counterintelligence operations within the base boundary to deny the enemy freedom of action

- When defending airbases; establishment of shoulder-launched surface-to-air-missiles suppression patrols and response capabilities to deny the enemy terrain from which to engage aircraft landing/taking off. This will be done within the base boundary or in coordination with the area commander.

Figure IV-3. Base Security Work Priorities

(e) Using the MSF to attack small enemy units threatening the base from within the base boundary.

(f) Providing internal security for critical capabilities and high value assets located on the base.

(g) Understanding established fire control measures to prevent fratricide within the base and between the bases and base clusters; as well as with other forces operating outside the base perimeter, to include the TCF, MSF, and HN security forces. In addition, the likelihood of civilians and infrastructure in the area around the base should be properly considered when deciding upon courses of action.

(2) The MSF commander must have the most up-to-date copy of the base defense plan, and, when applicable, base cluster defense plan in order to effectively coordinate between the base and MSF operations. This coordination occurs through the BDOC and

BCOC (if established). The MSF commander coordinates with the base to ensure that he understands the base defense plan, to include methods of contacting the BDOC or BCOC, including call signs and frequencies. Base defense plans and layouts should include the following:

      (a) Positions of critical internal assets, external coordination points, and no-fire areas.

      (b) Locations of any obstacles or mines near the base.

      (c) Locations and direction of fire of crew-served weapons.

      (d) Locations of target reference points and preplanned fires.

      (e) Locations of OPs employed by the base.

      (f) Signal for final protective fires.

      (g) How to obtain fire support and to clear fires.

      (h) Sensor and patrol plans.

      (i) Closest medical treatment facility.

Security forces should have a high degree of direct-fire lethality to cope with potential threats.

(j) Location of CBRN collective protection facilities and decontamination sites.

(k) Location of ammunition supply point.

(l) How to obtain aviation units tasked to respond to incidents.

(m) Communications plan.

(3) The composition and size of an MSF will vary. The nature and size of the threatening enemy force influences the size and number of MP, SF or land force combat arms elements that make up the MSFs. Base and base cluster commanders, in coordination with the JSC, consider the following:

(a) The priority of ongoing operations.

(b) The criticality of the base under attack.

(c) The amount of time needed for friendly elements to consolidate.

(4) The base commander, ICW the area commander, continuously assesses the situation and, if appropriate, requests commitment of more MSF assets to handle the threat.

b. **Control Measures.** Control measures in base and base cluster security operations are the same as those used in defensive operations. The JFC designates bases and base clusters. **The area commanders/base cluster commanders coordinate base boundaries, establish phase lines, contact points, objectives, and checkpoints as necessary to control the base clusters.** These control measures include fire support coordination measures (FSCMs) to permit or restrict fires in and around the base and base clusters. No-fire areas may be required to protect civilians, prevent disruption of sustaining operations, or protect combat outposts, OPs, and patrols. All control graphics are coordinated with HN agencies to minimize interference, misunderstandings, and unnecessary collateral damage. The base commander designates target reference points and sectors of fire for organizations located within the base boundary. All fires within the operational area will be coordinated among all affected organizations. These measures decrease the likelihood of fratricide, prevent noncombatant casualties, and minimize damage to the property of friendly civilians. The area commander normally designates reconnaissance and patrol areas to provide area security outside the base boundaries as necessary. MSFs must conduct aggressive patrols, and develop and occupy defensive positions in these areas in order to counter enemy attacks. The objective is to provide the base additional early warning, deter enemy actions and, if possible, defeat enemy elements operating in the base cluster. Areas should be assigned to cover all likely avenues of approach, areas likely to be used to launch stand-off weapons, and other key terrain.

c. **Base Security Tactics**

(1) **Defense Against Penetrating Attacks.** Perimeter primary positions must be prepared to prevent hostile forces from penetrating the base and interfering with its primary mission. If not capable of defeating enemy threats, the SF must delay the enemy until the MSF can respond. The base's MSF may be used to reinforce threatened areas, to block enemy penetrations of primary security positions, or to counterattack in order to regain lost security positions or destroy the attacking force. The MSF should be mounted in vehicles that provide as much personal protection as possible. SF should be equipped with reliable communications and should have sensors and devices to compensate for capability loss during periods of limited visibility. Aviation and naval support may be requested to augment the capabilities of base SF and enhance reconnaissance and surveillance operations. Sensors and defensive positions are employed on the base boundaries to provide indications and warning or detect and defeat the enemy. Joint fires are planned in detail to ensure the synchronization and integration of joint fire support capabilities, in support of the base defense and MSF. Forces (augmentation and selectively armed personnel) may be directed to secure facilities within the base vital to performance of the base's mission. Examples are the BDOC, ammunition storage areas, and aircraft revetments. SF require careful fire control to prevent fratricide.

(2) **Defense Against Standoff Attacks.** Standoff attackers are a fleeting target. Level I and II threats depend on blending in with the legitimate populace and only reveal themselves as combatants when they engage in a hostile act. It is not feasible to catch every terrorist or guerilla before they act, so the best practice is to shape the base security environment with robust defense operations within the base boundary.

(a) These proactive combat operations deny the enemy key terrain; disrupt enemy planning, reconnaissance, and organization; detect the enemy as they move into position; and posture forces to quickly neutralize detected forces.

(b) Robust tactical real-time ISR assets, to include HUMINT, within the base boundary can also act as a force multiplier to cue joint fires and forces. Some of these tactical ISR assets may also need to be located outside of the base boundary to provide early warning of threats and request area commander combat power to counter threats.

(c) For imminent threats originating outside the base boundary when the area commander is not able to assist due to competing priorities, the base commander must either use base security combat power to counter the threat with the permission of the area commander or assume the risk from enemy standoff attacks.

(d) The HN may also limit the base commander's ability to counter standoff attacks. In these cases, the use of joint patrols and/or liaisons officers may allow the base commander to affect their battlespace. Inability to adequately defend the base as a result of the host nation's limitations on the base boundary must be communicated up the chain of command to revise existing agreements or accept the risk

d. **Other Base Security Considerations**

(1) **Direct Fire Weapons Systems.** The base and/or port security force commanders should try to maximize the effectiveness of all available organic direct fire weapon system capabilities. Heavy direct fire weapons (often limited to heavy machine guns and automatic grenade launchers) must cover the most likely avenues of approach and have sufficient fields of fire to employ the weapons effectively and efficiently. Improvements to these positions should be continuous and range cards should be developed. If possible, in-place live fire training should be conducted. Often, civil considerations may limit the commander's authority to clear fields of fire and to conduct live fire training, especially if the base is adjacent to a major urban area.

(2) **Antiarmor Weapons.** Forces performing base security actions generally have few organic antiarmor weapons. Antiarmor weapons, including tanks, will be positioned to cover the most likely high-speed avenues of approach in mutually supporting positions. The base defense plan will assign positions for augmentation forces possessing antiarmor weapons.

(3) **Indirect Fire Systems.** Mortars, field artillery, and even naval surface fire can support the base security effort. In Level I and II threat environments, mortars are often the most readily available and most responsive indirect fire weapons systems.

(a) **Fire Support Planning.** The BDOC fire support officer is the focal point for the planning of indirect fires for base security. The BDOC fire support officer coordinates with the supporting fires cell (FC) or fire support coordination center (FSCC). Designated or planned targets should include areas likely to be used as locations for standoff weapons and likely enemy avenues of approach. **These targets should be planned to minimize collateral damage and civilian casualties.** Copies of fire support plans and target lists must be provided to the headquarters controlling the fire support assets. Targets may be planned outside the base boundary after coordination with the headquarters responsible for the area concerned. The BDOC and FSCC will ensure that all fire missions are properly coordinated to prevent the possibility of fratricide.

(b) **Fire Support Coordination Measures.** FSCMs permit or restrict fires in and around bases. Careful coordination must take place in planning these measures, especially with the HN. No-fire areas may be required to protect civilians or to prevent disruption of missions by friendly fire.

(c) **Observers.** Fire support units normally will not furnish observers to bases. Observers with appropriate training should be identified on each base to control supporting fires.

JP 3-09, Joint Fire Support, *and applicable Service publications provide additional information on fire support planning and FSCMs.*

(4) **Close Air Support (CAS).** The supporting FC or FSCC will maintain contact with the appropriate air control system to request CAS for base security efforts. When available, fixed- and rotary-wing aircraft and unmanned aircraft systems (UASs) may be used to extend the range of observation and provide immediate combat response to threats.

See JP 3-09.3, Close Air Support, *for more information on CAS.*

(5) **Other Aviation Support.** The BDOC and BCOC, with other C2 centers, coordinate other aspects of aviation support. Examples include air reconnaissance of the base or base cluster area and air movement of base security. They may also coordinate to manage air support priorities and diversions for emergency resupply, personnel augmentation, and evacuation.

(6) **Coastal and Harbor Security Support.** The supporting MESF commander will maintain contact with the maritime component commander to provide waterborne and shore security for seaports and bases that are adjacent to navigable waters, excluding air and missile security. When available, USCG and Navy coastal security resources may be used to extend the range of observation and provide immediate combat response to waterborne threats.

(7) **Vulnerability to Release of Toxic Industrial Materials (TIMs).** Base security planners must consider the threat of personnel TIM exposure due to TIM attack or accidental TIM release from adjacent industrial facilities such as chemical plants, nuclear power facilities, etc. Establish communications with industrial security forces for these facilities and a process for immediate notification of TIM release.

(8) **Barriers, Obstacles, and Mines.** The commander directs the construction and improvement of perimeter barriers. This includes establishing clear fields of fire and implementing physical security measures such as checkpoints on vehicle and pedestrian routes leading into the base, and port security units boarding suspect vessels. Concrete barriers, natural obstacles, and aggressive offensive actions can deny enemy access to the area immediately surrounding the base. Keeping the enemy at a distance degrades his ability to launch damaging attacks on the base. The commander should continue to direct improvement in the base defense, as time and other resources permit, to ensure a stable security system. Obstacles must be kept under observation and covered by direct and indirect fires. Some obstacles may be useful only for certain threat levels. For example, chain-link fencing may constitute a useful obstacle against Level I threats if well patrolled, but will be ineffective against higher-level threats. The use of mines will be very limited, if authorized at all.

See JP 3-15, Barriers, Obstacles, and Mine Warfare for Joint Operations, *and numerous Service publications for more information on barriers, obstacles, and mines.*

(9) **Physical Facilities.** Commanders must stress continuous upgrading for base physical security. Activities occupying fixed bases will have opportunities for installing sophisticated security equipment not available to units in mobile bases. Hardening of high

value areas within the base must be planned for, resources must be obtained, and actions carried out. Plans for base construction must consider ADC, fortification, survivability, and barrier/obstacles.

For more information on building standards, see Unified Facilities Criteria (UFC) 4-010-01, DOD Minimum Antiterrorism Standards for Buildings, *and the numerous Corps of Engineers Guidance Sheets.*

(a) **Intrusion Detection.** Defenders can place sensors on likely avenues of approach, locating them at the limits of the defense or outside the defense if coordinated with adjacent commands. Directed ground and sea surveillance radar and airborne forward-looking infrared systems, if available, can improve the chances of detecting intrusions early. Remotely monitored sensors, trip flares, binoculars, night vision devices, unmanned aircraft systems, and other nonlethal warning devices can also be useful. Dummy sensors at OPs and concealed surveillance resources also should be considered.

(b) **Observation.** To improve observation, defenders should clear the ground to the front of positions and from near perimeter fences by cutting foliage or applying defoliant. See JP 3-11, *Operations in Chemical, Biological, Radiological, and Nuclear (CBRN) Environments,* for more discussion. Perimeter roads on either side of the fence improve observation. A combination of concertina wire, lighting, surveillance cameras, and intrusion sensors enhances base security. Observation sites in guard towers or atop buildings can increase the surveillance capabilities of perimeter guards. In urban areas, leveling of adjacent buildings may be required, but these types of measures must be carefully weighed against the potential negative impact that they may have on the local civilian population.

(c) **Entrances.** The base should have as few entrances as possible. These entrances should meet existing CCDR and other published FP requirements. Control of the entrances must be balanced against threat and base mission requirements.

(d) **Working and Living Areas.** Buildings housing personnel and sensitive equipment should have adequate standoff from the perimeter as required by combatant command's standards and the UFC. Shelters with reinforced and sandbagged roofs should be near all working and living areas, to serve both as shelters and fighting positions.

For more information on building standards, see UFC 4-010-01, DOD Minimum Antiterrorism Standards for Buildings, *and the numerous Corps of Engineers Guidance Sheets.*

(e) **Medical Treatment Facilities.** Medical treatment facilities should be located and marked IAW the provisions of the Geneva Conventions. Medical units must not be used in an attempt to shield military objectives from attack and where possible should be so sited that attacks against military objectives do not imperil their safety. Base or base cluster commanders may direct otherwise only in circumstances dictated by operational imperatives. These commanders will seek authorization through the chain of command. Medical treatment facilities may be guarded by a picket or by sentries or by an escort. However, the guards are primarily to protect patients and medical personnel from marauders and bandits. Medical personnel are noncombatants and therefore shall not be employed in any combatant related duties.

(f) Base physical security plans must ensure adequate protection for mission essential vulnerable areas and task critical assets.

(10) **Operations Security (OPSEC) and Deception in Support of Operations Security.** OPSEC and deception operations must be integral to all planning and execution of any JSO. OPSEC and deception measures encompass several areas, some of which are; visual, sonic, electronic and olfactory (smell). Effective OPSEC and deceptive measures multiply the combat power of security operations by keeping the enemy ignorant of security activities and can cause him to act out of that ignorance, forcing him to make tactical, operational, or even strategic errors. Exploitation of those errors causes enemy plans and actions to fail, improving the overall security posture of the base or base cluster. OPSEC measures must be constant and effectively guarded to avoid compromise. Execution of good OPSEC demands that friendly security forces do not establish observable patterns, unless those patterns are part of a well-constructed deception plan. Deception measures must support the mission and be credible for the intended audience. Since deception does not occur without enemy observation, the commander must ensure that the enemy will interpret deceptive actions in a manner that is advantageous to the security plan.

For more information on OPSEC, see JP 3-13.3, Operations Security; *for more information on deception, see JP 3-13.4,* Military Deception.

(11) **Riverine Operations.** Rivers and other inland waterways provide significant transportation routes in much of the world. As such, security forces throughout the JSA may be called upon to either secure a river or inland waterway or utilize the waterway to secure the JSA itself. Additionally, riverine forces may be required to provide LOC security.

(12) **Nonlethal Weapons Systems.** Nonlethal weapons provide commanders with additional escalation-of-force options before having to resort to lethal force. These weapons should be fully considered in any base security plan to help minimize civilian casualties and property damage. A variety of nonlethal weapons exist to assist in discerning intent, delaying and deterring individuals, and discriminating targets in a variety of situations that occur in Level 1 threat environments.

5. Countering a Level III Threat

In some operations, there may be a conventional force Level III threat. In these situations, the JFC must consider and plan for combat operations in the JSA. Area commanders assigned a JSA as part of their AO must develop and organize TCFs and/or PSUs that are properly trained, led, and equipped to concentrate the necessary combat power at the decisive time and place. Defeating Level III threats within the JSA will ensure support bases can continue vital sustainment operations. Area commanders must also ensure that appropriate active and passive measures are taken in the JSA to protect US forces and equipment.

REAR AREA SECURITY — VIETNAM

Even though a "rear area" in Vietnam could not be defined by established linear boundaries, there were isolated pockets (de facto rear areas) that were considered to be relatively secure and yet found to be vulnerable to a determined enemy attack. The city of Saigon before the 1968 TET Offensive is an example. Saigon was an insulated city. Aside from occasional incidents of small-scale terrorism during more than 20 years of civil strife, the Communists had done little to disturb the sense of security enjoyed by most Saigonese. Defended by 10 Army of the Republic of Vietnam battalions and a division-sized national police force, and encircled by a series of major US command centers and bases, the capital seemed invulnerable to serious attack. TET would change that. Despite initial success, North Vietnamese attacks into the "rear area" eventually failed, but not before changing the course of the war.

SOURCE: Multiple Sources

---

a. **General.** Level III threats can result from enemy forces infiltrating or penetrating friendly positions and moving into the friendly operational area, or conducting airborne, air assault, or amphibious operations. The designated land force commander has several options to deal with the threat. The commander may establish a TCF to deal with such a threat; designate another force as the on-order TCF; or, accept the risk of not having a designated TCF. If required, the commander may establish a number of TCFs IAW the Level III threat and the JFC's guidance. Designating more than one TCF provides flexibility of response to competing needs. The primary advantage of having a dedicated, rather than an on-order, TCF is the assurance that the TCF can focus the force's planning and prepares activities for one mission. This includes establishing liaison and communications with supported bases and base cluster BDOCs and BCOCs. It also allows the dedicated TCF to rehearse its plans. When the designated commander assigns a subordinate unit an on-order TCF mission, there must be established criteria on when to commit that unit as the TCF. The tenets for successful combat operations in the JSA are knowledge of the enemy, unity of command, economy of force, and responsiveness.

b. **Tactical Combat Force.** Actual and potential Level III threats to the JSA may require the area commander to designate a TCF that can respond to the threat and protect the forces in the JSA. The area commander decides the composition of the TCF after weighing the risk of allocating forces to the TCF and thus decreasing the combat power available elsewhere. The size of a TCF will be based on METT-T. The TCF must be extremely mobile and capable of moving by air and ground because of limited reaction time and extended distances between units common to the JSA. It should be capable of defeating armored vehicles and dismounted infantry. Consequently, a TCF typically consists of infantry, Army or Marine Corps aviation (attack and utility helicopters), and air cavalry elements augmented with combat engineer and field artillery support. The commander may also organize a TCF with armored cavalry, armor, mechanized infantry units and naval attack aircraft and boats and vessels providing naval air and surface fire support if the situation so dictates. A TCF should have a full array of combat and combat support assets allocated to it to accomplish the mission. A TCF may have available support from the following types of assets:

(1) Military intelligence (includes CI).

(2) Field artillery.

(3) Engineers.

(4) Army or Marine Corps aviation (attack, air cavalry, air assault, C2, and possibly special electronic mission aircraft).

(5) MP/security police.

(6) CAS.

(7) Air defense artillery.

(8) Area signal nodes.

(9) Navy and USCG vessels and aircraft.

Any or all of these types of assets may not be immediately available to the TCF on its commitment. They are limited assets and may be engaged in other missions. The force conducting the JSA security mission may also receive support from other US and allied Services, including the HN.

c. **Responsibilities of the JFC.** The JFC's plans for combat actions in the JSA must be designed to optimize the use of all available US, multinational and/or HN forces. If determined that a TCF is warranted, the JFC (or designated representative) provides mission guidance to the responsible component or area commander owning the TCF.

d. **Responsibilities of the commander assigned the JSA within an AO.** The commander responsible for the security of the JSA will normally exercise TACON over the TCF. He ensures the TCF is properly established, trained, and supported. This commander normally will be responsible to coordinate TCF actions ICW the subordinate base cluster and commanders within the JSA.

e. **Responsibilities of the TCF commander.** The TCF will normally be under the C2 of the commander assigned the AO in which it is operating. MSFs designated by the JFC in the designated operational area may be placed under the TACON of the TCF commander. The TCF commander may also receive TACON of transient forces in an emergency, as directed by appropriate higher headquarters and IAW conditions established in JP 1, *Doctrine for the Armed Forces of the United States*. In addition, the TCF commander may receive joint fire support as directed by appropriate higher command. Finally, the TCF commander receives necessary liaison from component or other joint force commands (normally, liaison from component commands with area responsibilities comes from RAOCs or RTOCs).

f. **Base Security in Level III Threat Environments.** Bases are often very difficult to defend against Level III threats. When there is the possibility of a Level III threat against a base, extraordinary action may be required. These actions could include, but are not limited to:

(1) Significant additions to MSF capabilities.

(2) Employment of additional barriers and mines outside and around the base boundary.

(3) Developing extended, in depth individual defensive positions.

(4) Increased training and rehearsal of base defense actions to include rehearsal of MSF and TCF coordination.

(5) Enhanced fire support.

(6) Increased port security patrols.

(7) Improve integrated air and missile defense.

g. **Coordinating Base Defense and TCF Actions.** During Level III operations, the area commander retains overall C2 for security within the JSA. However, ICW the base/base cluster commander, the area commander may decide to delegate TACON over selected SF located in the TCF's operational area to the TCF commander, excluding air defense forces, which remain under the JFACC/AADC. These forces are used to delay and disrupt Level III threats, protect the flank of a TCF, or allow a base time to establish security in greater depth. Some base SF necessary for the protection of critical base assets may remain under the control of the base commander. MSF units within the perimeter work closely with the BDOC/BCOC to ensure a synchronized security plan is in place. BDOCs and/or BCOCs will establish and maintain contact with the tactical operations center of the area commander or the TCF as ordered. Upon notification by a base or base cluster commander through the BDOC or BCOC that a threat exceeds a base's security capabilities, the area commander may commit the TCF. The situation will dictate the C2 relationship between the security forces or TCF and the base security force as well as whether planned arrangements should be modified.

6. Air Base Defense Considerations

Air Base Approach and Departure Corridor Security. Aircraft are especially vulnerable when operating in the "low and slow" take-off and landing flight regimes. Air base approach and departure corridor security operations provide for the safety of aircraft from the shoulder-launched surface-to-air threat as they take off and land at air bases. Base commanders of any Service, who command installations with active airfields, must identify considerations for planning and securing air operations at airfields subject to threat systems. This should include approach and departure corridors used by the aircraft. They must also determine the best tactics, techniques, and procedures to counter and/or neutralize the surface-to-air threat, and identify seams within the joint force as they relate to securing aircraft arrivals and departures against surface-to-air threats. Threats to aircraft may be launched from a considerable distance from the air base. In the ideal case the base commander has sufficient forces attached and an appropriately sized base boundary to counter these threats. Base, base cluster, and area commanders must all be aware of the nature of these threats and share the responsibility to counter them.

a. **Planning.** Planning airfield approach and departure air corridor security requires the integration of air operations into the theater air plan, plotting shoulder-launched SAM footprints and defining approach and departure corridor security procedures. Air base commanders typically coordinate base boundaries with the area commander to ensure such boundaries provide appropriate protection for aircraft using approach and departure corridors. Depending on the air base capabilities, these areas may be within the base boundaries and the security provided by the base commander.

b. **Threats to Air Bases.** Airfield security and local area assessments should be conducted to identify the area of vulnerability to direct fire, indirect fire and shoulder-launched SAM threats (in terms of possible launch sites) to include the airfield arrival and departure corridors. A thorough assessment should include the capabilities of SF, intelligence, CI, and operational personnel as well as local/HN authorities.

(1) Criteria to identify possible direct fire, indirect fire and shoulder-launched SAM launch sites include but are not limited to:

(a) Cover and concealment — the ability of an object to conceal and prevent detection by friendly forces, and to provide protection for the adversary from return fire.

(b) Line of sight providing unobstructed view of the target.

(c) Exposure time — the amount of time the intended target is vulnerable from an operational attack.

(d) Distance to target and the range of the adversary's weapons systems as well as target recognition for the adversary to positively identify the intended target. Set up time required for an adversary's fire team to assemble into an attack position.

(e) The amount of time it takes to detect an adversary's fire team once their weapons are exposed.

(2) Because potential launch sites may be located some distance outside the existing base or installation fence-line, base commanders and area commanders must coordinate actions to protect airfields from attack. Actions include establishment of an appropriately delineated base boundary, defensive efforts and the allocation of resources to detect, deter, and destroy this threat to airfield operations and personnel.

(3) The preferred method is to deny an attacker access to potential launch sites, however that may not always be possible. Base, base cluster, and area commanders, depending on the situation, should develop and exercise contingency plans for responding to an incident of direct fire, indirect fire or shoulder-launched surface to air attack. Rapid reaction plans will facilitate the immediate engagement of an adversary attack or post-attack, to deter/prevent future attacks and ease concern for air travel safety by the public at large.

c. **Direct and Indirect Fire Threats**

(1) Vulnerability assessments should be conducted to identify the areas from which direct and indirect fire threats can attack lucrative ground targets such as mass gathering areas or parked aircraft.

(2) Consider dispersal of parked aircraft to reduce damage from direct or indirect fire attacks, such as rocket propelled grenades.

d. **Shoulder-Launched SAM System Threats**

(1) The Defense Intelligence Agency-Missile and Space Intelligence Center has flight path threat analysis simulation (FPTAS) software that allows the local commander to quantify the areas of greatest shoulder-launched SAM threat. FPTAS uses aircraft performance, flight path data, missile characteristics, and digital terrain elevation data to generate maps depicting areas from which shoulder-launched SAMs could engage US and allied aircraft. Commanders use these maps to identify flight paths with minimum exposure to the shoulder-launched SAM threat and to adjust take off/landing patterns to limit their exposure and use areas readily secured by ground troops. This software can be downloaded at the Defense Intelligence Agency-Missile and Space Intelligence Center website.

(2) Most CCDRs have designated their Air Force component as the office of primary responsibility for maintaining a database with current intelligence and operations information on select countries and airfields, to include a shoulder-launched SAM target acquisition. For example, Air Mobility Command (AMC), maintains the Virtual Threat Assessor. This database is used to determine the requirement for aircraft defensive systems to counter the shoulder-launched SAM threat; and on a more basic level, to determine whether nondefensive system equipped AMC military and commercial aircraft will be

permitted to operate into those countries or airfields. This information can assist the JFACC making their own policy decisions for aircraft operations at those same locations.

(3) There are two areas where commanders should employ mitigation measures to counter the shoulder-launched SAM threat: airfield/installation defense and reducing aircraft in-flight susceptibility.

(a) The following are points to consider in developing base defense plans in regard to airfield/installation defense and the shoulder-launched SAM threat.

1. Once an analysis of possible launch sites is accomplished, prime shoulder-launched SAM launch sites and vulnerable areas can be isolated by expanding the base boundary or airfield area of control and reducing areas of vulnerability. The following mitigation measures may require coordination with local/HN authorities:

a. Increased physical presence at prime launch sites. Visual observation of security teams is a strong deterrent.

b. Focused and random patrols of potential launch sites. Incorporate random patrols into the base defense plan.

c. Employment of technical equipment to detect and respond to the various threats.

2. Ensuring personnel are educated on the shoulder-launched SAM threat (to include component recognition), areas of vulnerability, and reaction plans. Develop and provide shoulder-launched SAM awareness training for security force personnel and local/HN authorities. Develop a shoulder-launched SAM awareness program for neighborhood watch groups and local business/installation facilities in close proximity to airfields or along flight paths. The Defense Intelligence Agency Missile and Space Intelligence Center has a web site in their Operation ENDURING FREEDOM section with a shoulder-launched SAM link that is a good source of information on shoulder-launched SAM systems.

(b) To reduce aircraft in flight susceptibility due to the shoulder-launched SAM threat, consider the following when developing base defense plans:

1. Establishing airfield specific procedures for the use of aircrew tactical countermeasures and/or tactics. Development and dissemination may require coordination with local/HN authorities. Ensure aircrew awareness of launch identification and the possible effect of shoulder-launched SAM on their aircraft. Ensure aircrews and flight operations are tied into the AMC intelligence combined risk assessment database to obtain current information on airfield security assessments.

<u>2.</u> Varying arrival and departure times of aircraft. Stagger the arrival times of normal scheduled missions to make arrival, departure, and ground times harder to predict for the adversary.

<u>3.</u> Randomly change approach and departure routes as a deterrent (IAW current Federal Aviation Administration guidelines).

<u>4.</u> Limit or discontinue use of landing lights within identified threat zones to reduce heat producing/targeting options.

<u>5.</u> In high threat areas or when intelligence has indicated a high alert status, coordinate, develop, and practice plans for engine-running offloads to minimize ground time.

e. **MSF Actions.** Command relationships; and tactics, techniques, and procedures must be identified to ensure MSF efforts are fully synchronized with air base operations in general.

7. Seaport Facility Defense Considerations

When a seaport or marine terminal is part of a formally designated base cluster, the base commander will normally be responsible for security within the base boundaries with HN, Army, or Marine Corps forces responsible for shore boundary defense and Navy and USCG forces providing waterside harbor approach security. However, if the seaport or marine terminal is isolated or located outside of a land combat area commander's AO, the designated HDC will normally be given responsibility to secure the seaport or marine terminal, as well as the harbor approaches. In these situations, the HDC may be required to use organic shore SF to serve as the MSF while other naval personnel provide boundary security. In other more high risk situations, the area commander, ICW the JSC and the HDC, may decide to provide a MSF from another Service for base security, especially if the seaport or marine terminal is isolated. In these situations, the MSF would be placed TACON to the HDC. The HDC should be aware that some arriving cargo ships may be carrying US Navy embarked security teams. These forces remain on the ship during loading/offloading operations and therefore are considered in the overall protection of the ship while in port.

Intentionally Blank

CHAPTER V
LINES OF COMMUNICATIONS SECURITY

> *"Co-equal with the security of flanks, the maintenance and full use of the lines of communications to the rear are of major concern to the commander. It is his responsibility that the incoming supply is equal to the needs of his deployments and that the supporting arms and fires which have been promised him keep their engagements. Or if they do not, he must raise hell about it."*
>
> **Brigadier General S.L.A. Marshall**
> **Men Against Fire**

1. Introduction

Successful onward movement of personnel, equipment, and materiel arriving in country (during joint reception, staging, onward movement, and integration) is vital to the success of joint force operations. In some operational environments, **the greatest risk to joint force operations may be the threat to the main supply routes (MSRs) from the ports of debarkation forward to the main battle area (in linear operations) or forward operating bases (in nonlinear, noncontiguous operations)**. This chapter provides guidelines for planning and executing surface LOC security operations in support of joint operations. This chapter also provides links between JSC LOC security actions with joint movement control operations.

2. Fundamentals of Lines of Communications Security

For the purposes of this publication, LOC **security operations include the protection of ground supply routes, inland waterways, rail lines and pipelines** that are used to support joint force operations in contingency operations (see Figure V-1). LOC security is especially challenging in major combat operations and in sustained, high risk combat and follow-on stability operations as seen in Operation IRAQI FREEDOM.

a. Security of LOCs that transit these nonassigned areas will require special consideration, especially in Level II and III threat environments. Even when the JFC designates a JSA, units may not have sufficient combat capabilities to adequately secure them.

b. **The key to successful LOC security is establishing and maintaining proper linkages throughout an operational area.** The commander designated with responsibility for the operational area is responsible for security. The JSC remains responsible to the JFC for coordination and staff oversight.

3. Joint Movement Control

a. The GCC has a wide range of options for performing successful joint movement control. Subordinate JFCs and Service components may be directed to carry out their own movement, or the GCC may establish a theater level joint transportation board. In some

FUNDAMENTALS OF
LINES OF COMMUNICATIONS SECURITY

► **LOC security is an operation, not a logistic function**

► **LOC security in Level II and III threat conditions will require dedicated security force capabilities**

► **LOC security actions must be closely synchronized with joint movement control operations**

LOC line of communications

Figure V-1. Fundamentals of Lines of Communications Security

instances a combination of both may exist. The organization charged with movement control plans, allocates, coordinates, and deconflicts transportation, as well as establishes and operates an in-transit visibility system to assist in tracking theater movements. It also establishes the location, identity, and communications facilities of nodes in the transportation system and promulgates tasking procedures, cycles, and deadlines. The joint movement control plan integrates the transportation capabilities of the component commands and provides for centralized planning and decentralized execution and is key to an effective movement control system. **Only through a disciplined joint movement control system can LOC security actions be properly planned for and executed.** The JSC must work closely with the designated joint movement control organization to ensure the movement control plan provides for movements to be conducted in a secure environment throughout the operational area.

b. The planning, routing, scheduling, control and security of personnel and cargo movement over LOCs throughout the operational area are vital to the support of the joint force. Normally, a JMC coordinates strategic movements with USTRANSCOM and in coordination with the JSC, oversees the execution of joint transportation priorities and controls movement actions. In major operations, the JMC executes movement control to include coordination of convoys passing through higher-level organizational, cross Service, and MNF boundaries.

(1) JSC links to the JMC ensures LOC security is maintained throughout the operational area. One viable technique to link the JSC and JMC planning functions is to establish a joint LOC security board (JLSB). Basic functions and characteristics of a JLSB can be found in Figure V-2.

(2) The JSC works closely with the JMC to monitor the security of joint movements throughout the operational area. The JSC may use assessment teams and recommend adjustment of security forces based on threats to movement security.

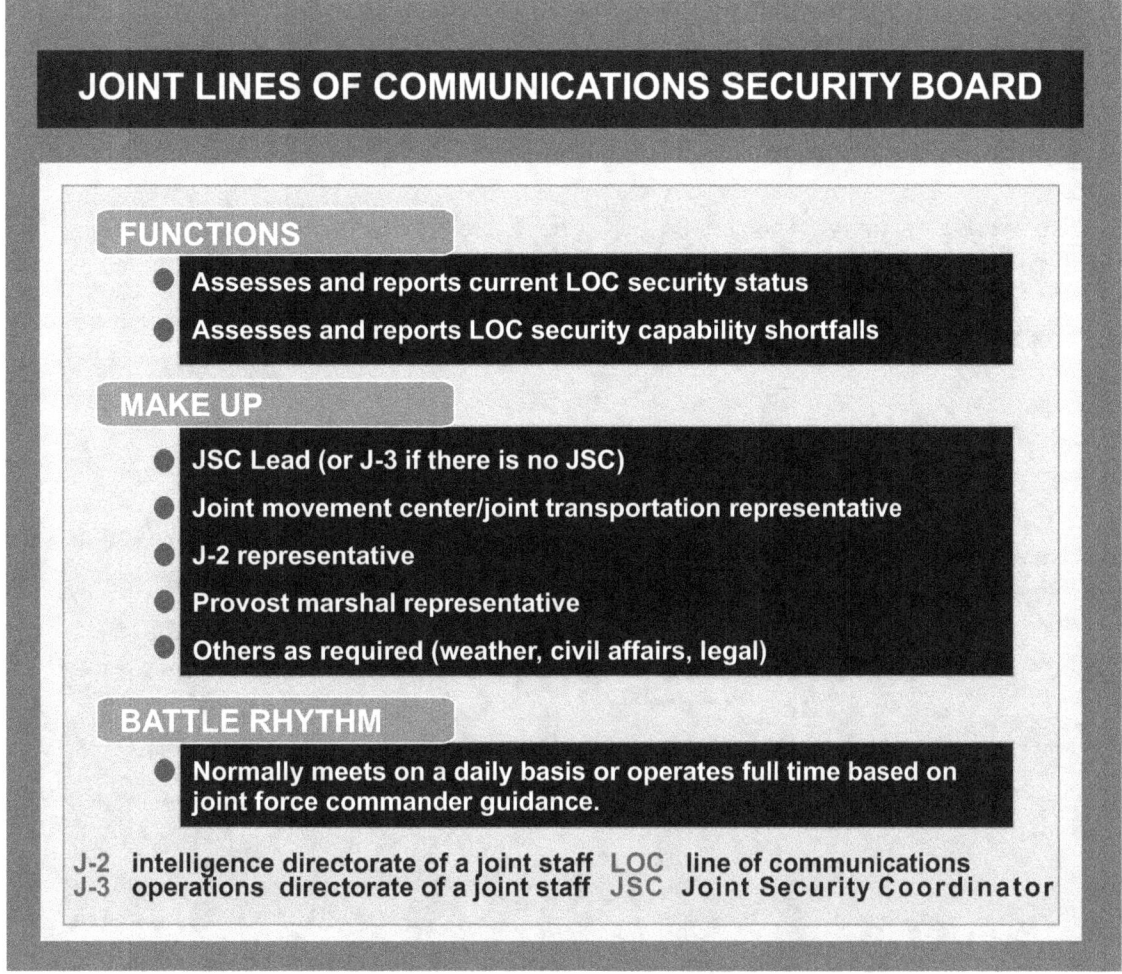

Figure V-2. Joint Lines of Communications Security Board

(3) A joint deployment and distribution operations center (JDDOC) is a joint capability solution designed to synchronize and optimize intertheater and theater deployment, distribution, and sustainment operations within a GCC's AOR. The JDDOC is an integrated operations and fusion center (movement control organization), acting in consonance with the GCC's overall requirements and priorities, and on behalf of the GCC, may direct common user and intratheater distribution operations. The JMC will work closely with the JDDOC.

For further information on movement control see JP 4-0, Joint Logistics, *and JP 4-09,* Distribution Operations.

4. **Security of Lines of Communications**

The primary threats to movement along ground LOCs in Level I and II threat environments are mines, ambushes, IEDs and VBIEDs. IEDs and VBIEDs may incorporate chemical or radiological material to create exposure and contamination hazards. Level III threats may include risk from air and ground conventional force interdiction.

Land LOCs, rail lines and pipelines may also be vulnerable to demolitions, sniper fire, and indirect fire. Commanders and their staff develop LOC security requirements and identify appropriate risk mitigation measures to ensure LOCs remain open. Logistic personnel should synchronize these measures with joint security operations. Certain units, such as NAVELSG, rely on the supported commander to provide force protection.

a. **Active Security.** The active LOC security techniques include measures initiated to achieve positive control of the LOCs and reduce the threat. Active security includes:

    (1) Patrols.

Land forces provide cordon security along a main supply route during Operation IRAQI FREEDOM.

    (2) Snipers.

    (3) Fighting positions along LOCs.

    (4) Check points.

    (5) Route sweeps.

b. **Cordon Security Operations.** Cordon security operations are **area defense missions that support a specific route for a designated period during which multiple movements take place**. They are used to establish a security cordon in order to allow safe passage for personnel, accompanying materiel and/or units transiting high-risk portions of the operational area. Cordon security requires appropriate land combat arms capabilities and other resources to properly observe and secure the designated route. Cordon operations may be used to establish a reserved route that is used exclusively by military or designated USG and NGO support actions. The JFC must consider the resources and possible negative civil impact of this particular LOC security operation.

(1) **Movement Corridors.** Commanders typically use a variety of tactics, techniques, and procedures to complement LOC security operations. One such procedure is the establishment of movement corridors. A movement corridor is established to a secure ground LOC that connects two or more support areas within the operational area that complements cordon security operations and is part of a layered and integrated security approach to LOCs. A layered security typically normally consists of a number concentric rings that provide increased survivability and response measures. The width and depth of the movement corridor will be dependant on METT-T and the GCCs' guidance.

(2) Security cordons protect the LOCs by keeping enemy forces more focused on the security force than on engaging vulnerable forces moving along the LOCs. Cordon security is provided by two or more combat outposts positioned to provide mutual support. The JSC, via the JFC's J-3, normally assigns a specific area commander with responsibility for this mission. The area commander uses selected air assault, mechanized, or motorized combat units to man combat outposts at critical locations along the assigned route. Notionally, a combat outpost would be composed of a mechanized or motorized platoon-size element equipped with automatic weapons, communications, and sensors and would be supported by dedicated fire support assets. Outpost and patrol duties are performed on a rotational basis. On waterway LOCs, motorized land forces may not be available or may not be sufficient to provide the cordon. In this case, patrol boats armed in similar fashion would provide or reinforce security.

(3) One of the primary responsibilities of the cordon commander is to collect and disseminate route combat information. This information is provided to higher headquarters, the JSC and all units moving or scheduled to move along the designated route. In some cordon operations, the cordon outposts may also serve as communications relay sites.

(4) Combat outposts are located within supporting distance of each other whenever possible. Units assigned to these combat outposts provide MSFs in the event of enemy activity along the route within their assigned cordon. Forces based at these combat outposts conduct random or directed reconnaissance patrols, UAS sorties, and/or offensive operations to counter enemy activities between these two points on a frequent but irregular schedule. If available, rotary- or even fixed-wing aircraft may be used to assist in cordon security operations. The presence of rotary- or fixed-wing assets can provide significant enhancements to LOC security.

c. **Passive Security.** Passive LOC security techniques include measures initiated to achieve security without a significant expenditure of manpower or resources. Passive LOC security techniques include the following.

(1) Formation and march control of convoys with convoy security so they present the least lucrative target possible under prevailing conditions.

(2) Security related driving techniques (speed of march, actions on contact, overwatch positions).

(3) Proper selection of routes.

(4) Variations of convoy departure times.

(5) OPSEC measures.

(6) Capitalizing on security offered by other activities not related to the LOC's security requirements enhance security along LOCs. These activities include aircraft traversing the LOC, maintenance activities taking place along the LOC, training exercises or troop movements adjacent to or along the LOC, HN military and police traffic control activities, and the activities of the civilian population. The commander uses passive security for all conditions or situations and as an adjunct to any other technique of LOC security employed. They are the products of a long-term and continually improved program for an integrated security system.

For more information on convoy operations, see FM 4-01.45/Marine Corps Reference Publication (MCRP) 4-11.3H/NTTP 4-01.3/Air Force Tactics, Techniques, and Procedures (AFTTP) 3-2.58, Multi-Service Tactics, Techniques, and Procedures for Tactical Convoy Operations.

d. **Reconnaissance and Surveillance.**   LOC reconnaissance and surveillance addresses not only MSRs, pipelines and waterways, but may include the terrain along the LOCs that the enemy could use to influence the joint force's movement. LOC reconnaissance and surveillance takes place at irregular intervals to avoid developing a regular pattern that an enemy force could exploit. Route reconnaissance and surveillance techniques can include the following:

(1) Use of manned aircraft or UASs.

(2) HN military or police physical reconnaissance/traffic control actions.

LINES OF COMMUNICATIONS — IRAQ

In the spring of 2004, insurgents destroyed seven vital bridges along the main supply routes in Iraq. The unexpected loss of these bridges led to serious supply shortages until bypasses were found and repairs were made.

SOURCE: Various Open Sources

---

(3) Coordinating combat arms land force patrols and other actions, along selected LOCs.

(4) Waterway patrols.

5. Other Considerations

a. **Risk Management.** The JFC, normally through a JSC, uses the risk management process and the JLSB (if established) as well as directs staff coordination process to assess risk to LOC security. The JSC works closely with the JFC's J-2, J-3, and logistics directorate of a joint staff/JMC and other key special staff elements and component representatives, HN, other US agencies, and MNFs to determine risk to LOC security and measures to defeat or mitigate these risks. The JSC must ensure there is a dedicated process to assist commanders and staffs at all levels to reduce, mitigate, or defeat risks to forces transiting surface LOCs. LOC security planning must be linked directly to the JFC JIPOE process and updates must be disseminated and shared as they are identified. The JSC identifies risk, develops potential courses of action, assesses and addresses resource requirements, implements the actions (through subordinate commanders) and then monitors the LOC security actions. The specific steps in the risk management process are: identify threats, assess threats to determine risk, develop control or security measures, make risk assessment decisions, implement control and security measures, and review these measures for continued use.

SUPPLY ROUTE TAMPA

In Operation IRAQI FREEDOM, US Army military police forces were used to provide limited route security along main supply route TAMPA from the border of Kuwait north to the northern Iraqi city of Mosul. A key part of this mission was to provide tactical communication relay capability. This nontraditional mission was required due to the length and criticality of the main supply routes as well as the lack of other communications options.

SOURCE: Army Transportation Battalion Commander's
End-of-Tour Report

---

b. **Civil Considerations.** The JFC, normally through the JSC, must be careful to take civil considerations into account when planning LOC security related actions. LOC security actions can and will have an effect on the civilian population as well on other USG and NGO support actions in the operational area. In some instances, the JFC may determine it is necessary to temporarily designate a route for military use only. This decision has the potential to have a negative impact on the local population as well as USG and NGO support actions. Even if the JFC does not fully restrict a route from civilian traffic, LOC security actions can have a negative impact. It is imperative that all LOC security related decisions be coordinated with the JFC CMO staff.

For further information on CMO, see Chapter III, "Planning," and JP 3-57, Civil-Military Operations.

c. **Communications and Reporting Requirements.** In a joint environment, regulation of transportation and LOC security will prevent congestion and enforce the LOC security plan. Robust and well-planned communications and reporting requirements must be planned for and resourced. Often, resources to support LOC are unreliable and/or unavailable and may require reallocation of available communications resources by the JFC communications system directorate of a joint staff. Joint transportation planners must determine which LOC requires joint control and which ones will be regulated via area commanders. The traffic regulation reporting plan must be coordinated with and support LOC security requirements. To accomplish successful movement, the transportation system must be linked to an information and communications system, to include the JSC and his staff on behalf of the JFC. These systems provide data in time to adjust the responses of the terminals and nodes along LOCs. In some cases, a dedicated LOC security frequency may be designated. In extreme cases, the Joint Surveillance Target Attack Radar System may be used to assist in the LOC security mission.

APPENDIX A
JOINT SECURITY OPERATIONS CENTERS

1. **Joint Security Coordination Center**

   a. **JSCC Basic Functions.** The JSCC conducts 24-hour operations and its primary responsibilities include, but are not limited to the following.

   (1) Coordinate and oversee overall current and future security operations within the AOR and/or the JOA. Monitor emergency service, FP, AT, physical security, base and base cluster defense plans, and FPWG policies, plans, and operations to ensure applicability with operation plans, orders, directives, policies, and regulations.

   (2) Ensure the JFC's operational vulnerability assessment and assistance program (VAAP) provides assistance and advice on risk mitigation measures to all bases, base clusters, LOCs, APODs, SPODs, and other organizations or facilities located in the AOR and/or the JOA.

   (3) Prepare policy, plans and guidance on JSO for implementation by subordinates assigned within an AOR and/or the JOA.

   (4) Assist the J-3 in the preparation of joint security plans and orders relating to current operations. When necessary, coordinate with the J-3 in order to deconflict specific JSO with on-going, planned operations.

   (5) Keep the JSC informed of the current situation within the AOR and/or the JOA and apprised of all joint security operations, including enemy, friendly, and civilian activities.

   (6) Monitor the current status of assigned or attached security forces and other resources and provide information to aid, allocate, and move forces and material as necessary.

   (7) Ensure the participation of units within the AOR and/or the JOA in conducting active and passive security measures to include integration of the IADS.

   (8) Identify and prioritize allocation of resources to defeat or mitigate vulnerabilities.

   (9) Provide for centralized collection and processing of information from various intelligence and operational sources and disseminating and sharing resultant intelligence products to include all joint security related base and LOC threat conditions, weather, hazards, etc.

   (10) As required, provide members to JLSB (if JLSB is stood up).

(11) Prepare operational reports as required; also maintain a staff journal, display and file necessary items to record operational activities of the joint command.

b. **Unique Positions and Responsibilities Within the JSCC**

(1) **Joint Security Coordinator.** Principal staff officer responsible for the planning and preparation of JSO throughout the operational area.

(2) **Chief of Staff / Deputy, Joint Security Coordinator.** Assistant to the JSC for the planning and preparation of JSO throughout the operational area. Responsible for coordinating actions and directing the JSCC staff for the JSC.

2. Base Defense Operations Center

Basic BDOC Functions. The BDOC conducts 24-hour operations and its primary functions include, but are not limited to the following.

a. Provide the C2 organization necessary to conduct coordinated base security operations.

b. Prepare plans to implement the base commander's overall base defense guidance.

c. Plan and execute FP, AT, and physical security operations IAW published guidance.

d. Conduct FPWG and threat working group.

e. Monitor the current status of assigned, attached, and tenant unit forces and resources and provide information to aid, allocate, and move forces and material to meet base defense requirements.

f. Identify and communicate any base defense shortfalls to the base cluster commander or JSC, as well as Service or applicable functional component command.

g. Keep the base commander informed of the current base security situation.

h. Ensure the participation of all units within the base perimeter in conducting active and passive security measures. Monitor and direct guard forces as necessary.

i. Assess potential conflicting interests and operational demands of base forces inherent when operating in multi-Service or multinational environment.

j. Develop and execute a reconnaissance and surveillance plan to ensure proper security from standoff threats within base boundaries and coordinate with area commander/base cluster commander to for the area outside the base boundary.

k. Establish and maintain connectivity with higher-level staff (BCOC or JSCC).

l. Prepare security related operational reports as required; also maintain a staff journal, display and file necessary items to record operational activities of the command.

m. When necessary, coordinate with the appropriate area commander or tenant commander to ensure that base security actions are deconflicted with ongoing or planned combat or stability operations.

n. Plan and coordinate the base fire support plan.

o. Identify and share base emergency response/ADC capabilities to include medical support, combat engineering, EOD, fire fighting, etc.

p. Evaluate actions to identify operational deficiencies and develop methods to improve combined operational effectiveness to include coordinating training and exercising base security measures.

3. Base Cluster Operations Center

Basic BCOC Functions. The BCOC acts as both a BDOC and BCOC, so it would perform all basic functions and specific BDOC tasks described above. Additional BCOC functions would include, but are not limited to the following.

a. Keeping the base cluster commander informed of the current situation within his base cluster, including enemy, friendly, and civilian activities.

b. Preparing comprehensive plans to implement the base commander's overall base cluster defense and security guidance.

c. Communicating any base defense shortfalls identified to the JSC, as well as Service component and/or applicable functional component command.

d. Assessing potential conflicting interests and operational demands of base cluster forces inherent when operating in multi-Service or multinational environment.

e. Providing centralized collection and processing of information from various intelligence and operational sources and sharing resultant base cluster intelligence products as appropriate. Information would include weather, civil considerations, LOC conditions, CBRN threats, IEDs, or other know hazards.

f. Providing the essential C2 organization to conduct integrated base defense.

g. Developing and executing a reconnaissance and surveillance plan to ensure that bases are properly protected from stand-off threats outside their base boundary.

h. Establishing and maintaining connectivity with higher level staff (JSCC or JSC).

i. When necessary, coordinating and deconflicting base security, base cluster security, and local combat operations.

j. Planning and coordinating the base cluster fire support plan.

k. Identifying and sharing base and base cluster emergency response and ADC capabilities to include medical support, combat engineering, EOD, fire fighting, etc.

l. Evaluating actions to identify operational deficiencies and develop methods to improve combined operational effectiveness to include coordinating training and exercising base defense measures.

4. **Common Positions and Key Responsibilities for all Operations Centers**

The following positions, when created, normally require personnel to be dual hatted:

a. **Operations Officer.** The operations officer serves as the principal advisor to the JSC or base commander on all operational matters. Other responsibilities include the following.

(1) Direct the operations within the center.

(2) Develop a training, exercise, and certification plan for the JSCC staff, or units and individuals who have been designated as part of the base defense plan.

(3) Monitor current operations and intelligence in order to help synchronize the efforts and make operational decisions in line with the JSC/base commander's intent. Enforce full participation and support to the FPWG and VAAP.

(4) Seek guidance from the principal staff on situations that are beyond the operations officer's decision-making authority.

(5) Notify staff sections on significant operational events and include appropriate staff sections in critical decisionmaking.

(6) Prepare and submit operational and situational reports as required to the JSC/base commander.

(7) Monitor outgoing communications and correspondence for completeness, accuracy, and staff coordination.

(8) Maintain a log of significant events and distribute the guidance from the JSC/base commander or staff officers.

(9) Coordinate planning with higher headquarters.

(10) Monitor security status of base(s) and deconflict security operations.

(11) Assist in developing priority intelligence requirements and coordinating with appropriate staffs for collection on intelligence requirements.

b. **Intelligence Officer.** The intelligence officer's duties are listed below.

(1) Supervise intelligence section personnel.

(2) Ensure frequent communications with higher-level intelligence organization as directed by the JSC.

(3) Provide intelligence input on the situation report (SITREP).

(4) Ensure subordinate commands receive intelligence updates and other information in a timely manner through the most appropriate means.

(5) Ensure maps are ordered and distributed.

(6) Provide daily intelligence update to the operations center and FPWG.

(7) Coordinate and maintain liaison with HN intelligence agencies.

(8) Keep the Operations Officer informed of all significant intelligence and intelligence action and events.

c. **Force Protection Officer.** This officer serves as the principle advisor to the JSC or base commander on all AT, FP, physical security, and emergency services matters. Duties include the following:

(1) Develop, publish, and provide guidance on all FP, AT, physical security, vulnerability assessment, and working group policies and procedures.

(2) Chair the JSC/base commander's FPWG and threat working group.

(3) Assist the operations officer to prepare and submit operational and situational reports as required to the base commander.

(4) Brief the operations officer on FP matters.

(5) Set the standard for the base commander's FPWG, to include ensuring unity of effort on base defense; sharing of information and intelligence; establishing the FPWG's agenda, priorities, and VAAP input; conduct and monitor the JSC/base commander's risk assessment program; and identify base defense resources.

d. **Battle Captain.** The battle captain will:

(1) Be responsible for tracking day-to-day operations.

(2) View all incoming messages and distribute appropriate guidance for each.

(3) Act as the operational focal point in coordinating the efforts of the staff.

(4) Ensure the accuracy of map information, mission statement, task organization charts, battle board information, the significant events display and daily journal.

(5) Provide daily operational update to the FPWG.

(6) Determine which events appear on the significant event display.

(7) Inform other staff sections of significant events.

(8) Monitor the communications network ICW the communications noncommissioned officer (NCO).

(9) Direct or commence the drafting of required operational action messages such as fragmentary orders

(10) Coordinate the shift change briefings.

(11) Monitor the progress of the base commander's daily SITREP to ensure all required inputs are received in a timely manner to allow the message to be transmitted on time.

e. **Operations NCO.** The operations NCO's primary duties include the following.

(1) Assist the operations officer in the conduct of operations.

(2) Assist with the accuracy of map information, mission statement display, task organization chart, chart data board information, maintain the journal, and ensure the situation map is up to date.

(3) Maintain master files for all incoming and outgoing messages by date time group.

(4) Maintain the significant events log.

(5) Ensure files, logs and reports (both computer and hard copy) are maintained, current, and submitted as required.

(6) Supervise information flow procedures.

(7) Supervise the maintenance of incoming and outgoing message files and ensure message read files are available for the base commander and staff.

(8) Provide direct supervision of the daily journal.

(9) Establish personnel and equipment listings for administrative support.

(10) Be responsible for the routine upkeep and maintenance of the operation center.

(11) Assist in the daily preparation of the SITREP.

(12) Obtain material required by the staff.

(13) Prepare map overlays as required.

   f. **Fire Support Officer.** The fire support officer's duties include the following.

(1) Assist the operations officer to develop base fire support plans.

(2) Coordinate fire support related plans, measures, and communications requirements with the appropriate BDOC, BCOC, JSCC staff, or area command staff as required.

(3) Conduct assessments of existing fire support plans and coordinate exercise/rehearsals of same.

   g. **Communications Officer.** When there is no full-time communications officer, then the operations NCO would serve in this position. Key duties include:

(1) Provide advice on communications matters.

(2) Ensure adequate secure voice and communications connectivity is maintained with appropriate headquarters.

(3) Coordinate required communications for the JSCC/BDOC/BCOC.

(4) Maintain a log of significant communications activities.

(5) Monitor action on all communications operations.

(6) Prepare briefings on communications status for the JSC/base commander and provide communications input to the SITREP.

(7) Maintain the secure telephone system between higher and subordinate command headquarters.

(8) Maintain current status of all joint communications in support of the operation and available for contingency operations.

(9) Identify trends that may develop to degrade communications.

(10) React to requests for additional communications support, or restoration of degraded communications.

(11) Publish telephone number listing.

(12) Actively participate in and support the FPWG and VAAP.

h. **Logistics Officer.** The logistics officer's duties include the following.

(1) Maintain a thorough knowledge and understanding of all logistic plans and actions applicable to base defense requirements.

(2) Monitor and coordinate the logistic functions and requirements, including general engineering, in support of base defense.

(3) Prepare logistic input to the SITREP.

(4) Actively participate and support the FPWG and VAAP.

i. **Engineer.** The engineer officer's duties include:

(1) Advise and establish JSC/base commander's general engineering policy and guidance.

(2) Provide general engineering and when applicable, combat engineering and input to JSC/base defense plans.

(3) Coordinate and supervise base defense construction and environmental support actions.

(4) Develop infrastructure criteria IAW the JFC engineer guidance.

(5) Coordinate for the contract procurement of real property FP equipment (i.e., barriers, guard shacks, lighting).

(6) Actively participate and support the FPWG and VAAP.

j. **CBRN Officer.** The CBRN officer will:

(1) Act as lead subject matter expert for CBRN defense, response to CBRN incidents, and sensitive site exploitation.

(2) Actively participate and support FPWG.

(3) Conduct vulnerability analysis based on the latest intelligence/threat assessments.

(4) Assist operations officer in devising CBRN defense plans and review CBRN annexes to higher headquarters operation plan and concept plan.

(5) Support the operations center for theater-level CBRN warning and reporting.

(6) Coordinate with medical representative on health support requirements.

(7) Coordinate with logistics officer pertaining to chemical defense equipment, supplies, maintenance, and transportation of CBRN defense assets.

k. **Medical Representative.** The medical representative's duties include:

(1) Advise JSC/base commander and staff on health service support matters related to base defense.

(2) Plan for and assist in exercising mass casualty treatment.

(3) Plan for and assist in exercising base casualty evacuation procedures.

(4) Actively participate and support the FPWG and VAAP.

l. **Liaison Officers.** Represent respective tenant units, component, and/or activity. Actively participate in all planning and actively participate in the FPWG and VAAP as required.

Intentionally Blank

APPENDIX B
SAMPLE BASE DEFENSE PLAN

1. **Overview**

a. The format outlined below is offered as one method of developing a sample base defense plan. It is optimized for a base or installation, to include deployed units and can be adapted for use at other facilities. It is meant to help the JSC, as the principal staff officer responsible for planning and preparation of JSO throughout the operational area, structure the base defense plan in a comprehensive and organized manner. The format is patterned after the standard five-paragraph military operation order (Situation-Mission-Execution-Administration and Logistics-Command and Signal).

b. This format enables the integration of existing programs such as law enforcement, physical security, AT, OPSEC, information security, high-risk personnel protection, and other installation efforts. Base defense plans should be integrated into all plans and separate annexes. Remember that staff interaction is a crucial element of developing a realistic, executable plan.

c. Although this sample is patterned after the military operation order, it can be used by other DOD agencies and facilities to protect personnel, activities, and material under their control.

d. This sample uses supporting annexes, appendices, tabs, and enclosures to provide amplifying instructions as required. This method shortens the length of the basic plan (which should be read by all personnel outlined in the plan), and provides organization, structure, and scalability.

e. The primary reference for plan formats is Chairman of the Joint Chiefs of Staff Manual (CJCSM) 3122.03C, *Joint Operation Planning and Execution System Volume II, Planning Formats.* Should a conflict exist between this Appendix and the format found in CJCSM 3122.03C, the Joint Operation Planning and Execution System manual format takes precedence.

2. **Sample Format**

> (In Joint Operation Order Format)
> SECURITY CLASSIFICATION
> Copy No. _____
> Issuing Headquarters
> Place of Issue
> Message Reference Number

Type and Serial Number of Operation Order.

References:

    a. Maps or Charts

    b. Time Zone. (Insert the time zone used throughout the order)

Task Organization. (List this information here, in paragraph 3, or in an annex if voluminous. The organization for defense should clearly specify the base units providing the forces for each defense element. Attached or transient units and the names of commanders should be included. The defense requirements of US, HN, and other civilian organizations quartered on the base also should be identified. Their capabilities to assist in the defense must be determined and integrated into the base defense plan.)

1. Situation. (Under the following headings, describe the environment in which defense of the base will be conducted, in sufficient detail for subordinate commanders to grasp the way in which their tasks support the larger mission.)

    a. Enemy Forces. (Describe the threat to the base, to include the composition, disposition, location, movements, estimated strengths, and identification and capabilities of hostile forces, including terrorist organizations.)

    b. Friendly Forces. (List information on friendly forces not covered by this operation order, to include the mission of the next higher headquarters and adjacent bases as well as units not under base command whose actions will affect or assist the defense of the base. These units may include MP or Air Force SF response forces, fire support, naval coastal warfare forces, special operations forces, engineers, decontamination or smoke units, EOD, HN military or police organizations, and public and private civilian organizations of both the United States and HN.)

    c. Attachments or Detachments. (When not listed in the Task Organization, list elements attached to or detached from base units and the effective times.)

2. Mission. (Give a clear, concise statement of the commander's defense mission.)

3. Concept of the Operation. (Under the following headings, describe the commander's envisioned concept of the operation.)

    a. Commander's Intent. (The commander discusses how the development of the defense is envisioned and establishes overall command priorities. This subparagraph should provide subordinates sufficient guidance to act upon if contact is lost or disrupted.)

    b. Concept of Operation. (Briefly describe how the commander believes the overall operation should progress. Define the areas, buildings, and other facilities considered critical, and establish priorities for their protection.)

(1) Phasing. (Set forth, if necessary, the phases of the operation as they are anticipated by the commander.)

(2) Maneuver. (Describe the organization of the ground defense forces, the assignment of elements to counter standoff and penetrating attacks to include the base boundary patrol concept of operation and establishment of a defense with primary, alternate, and supplementary defensive positions, as well as reaction force responsibilities. Describe the purpose of counterattacks and set work priorities.)

(3) Fires. (State plans for employing air and missile defense and supporting fires, such as mortars and other indirect fire assets, smoke, and aviation support.)

c. Tasks for Subordinate Elements. (If not previously described, this and succeeding subparagraphs should set forth the specific tasks for each subordinate defense element listed in the Task Organization.)

d. Reserve. (The next-to-last subparagraph of paragraph 3 contains instructions to the base's mobile reserve.)

e. Coordinating Instructions. (Always the last subparagraph of paragraph 3. Contains those instructions applicable to two or more elements or to the command as a whole.)

(1) Control Measures. (Define and establish restrictions on access to and movement into critical areas. These restrictions can be categorized as personnel, materiel, and vehicles. Security measures also may be outlined here.)

(a) Base Boundary. (Define and establish the base boundary as coordinated with the area commander. Include a description of plans to cope with enemy standoff attacks.)

(b) Personnel Access. (Establish control pertinent to each area or structure.)

1. Authority. (Give authority for access.)

2. Criteria. (Give access criteria for unit contractor personnel and local police and armed forces.)

3. Identification and Control

a. (Describe the system to be used in each area. If a badge system is used, give a complete description to disseminate requirements for identification and control of personnel who conduct business on the base.)

b. (Describe how the system applies to unit personnel, visitors to restricted or administrative areas, vendors, contractor personnel, and maintenance and support personnel.)

(c) Materiel Control Procedures

1. Incoming

a. (List requirements for admission of materiel and supplies.)

b. (List special controls on delivery of supplies to restricted areas.)

2. Outgoing

a. (List required documentation.)

b. (List special controls on delivery of supplies from restricted areas.)

c. (List classified shipments.)

(d) Vehicle Control

1. (State policy on registration of vehicles.)

2. (State policy on search of vehicles.)

3. (State policy on parking.)

4. (State policy on abandoned vehicles.)

5. (List controls for entering restricted areas.)

(e) Train Control

1. (State policy on search of railcars.)

2. (State policy on securing railcars.)

3. (State policy on entry and exit of trains.)

(2) Security Aids. (Indicate the manner in which the following security aids will be implemented on the base.)

(a) Protective Barriers

1. Definition.

2. Clear zones.

     <u>a.</u> Criteria.

     <u>b.</u> Maintenance.

  <u>3.</u> Signs.

     <u>a.</u> Types.

     <u>b.</u> Posting.

  <u>4.</u> Gates.

     <u>a.</u> Hours of operation.

     <u>b.</u> Security requirements.

     <u>c.</u> Lock security.

     <u>d.</u> Protective lighting system. (Use and control, inspection, direction, actions during power failures, emergency lighting.)

  (b) Intrusion Detection System

     <u>1.</u> Types and locations.

     <u>2.</u> Security classifications.

     <u>3.</u> Maintenance.

     <u>4.</u> Operation.

     <u>5.</u> Probability of Detection.

       <u>a.</u> Limitations.

       <u>b.</u> Compensating measures.

       <u>c.</u> Redundant capabilities.

  (3) Interior Guard Procedures. (Include general instructions that apply to all interior guard personnel, fixed and mobile. Attach detailed instructions such as special orders and standing operating procedures as annexes. Ensure that procedures include randomness.)

(a) Composition and organization. (NOTE: In security and support operations environment, the interior guard may be a contracted civilian security force.)

(b) Tour of duty.

(c) Essential posts and routes.

(d) Weapons and equipment.

(e) Training.

(f) Military working dogs.

(g) Method of challenge.

(h) Alert force.

1. Composition.

2. Mission.

3. Weapons and equipment.

4. Location.

5. Deployment concept.

(4) Rules of Engagement. (Delineate the circumstances and limitations under which US forces will initiate and/or continue combat engagement with other forces encountered.)

(5) Contingency Plans. (Indicate actions in response to various emergency situations. List as annexes any detailed plans, such as combating terrorism, responding to bomb threats and hostage situations, dealing with disasters, and firefighting.)

(a) Individual actions.

(b) Alert force actions.

(6) Security Alert Status.

(7) Air Surveillance.

(8) Noncombatant Evacuation Operation Plans.

(9) Coordination with HN or Adjacent Base Plans.

(10) Measures for Coordination with Response Force and Tactical Combat Forces.

(11) Procedures for Update of This OPORD. (If the OPORD is not effective upon receipt, indicate when it will become effective.)

4.   Administration and Logistics. (This paragraph sets forth the manner of logistic support for base defense. State the administrative and logistic arrangements applicable to the operation. If the arrangements are lengthy, include them in an annex or a separate administrative and logistics order. Include enough information in the body of the order to describe the support concept.)

a. Concept of Combat Service Support. (Include a brief summary of the base defense concept from the combat service support point of view.)

b. Materiel and Services. (List supply, maintenance, transportation, construction, and allocation of labor.)

c. Medical Services. (List plans and policies for treatment, hospitalization, and evacuation of both military and civilian personnel.)

d. Damage Control. (List plans for firefighting, clearing debris, and emergency construction.)

e. Personnel. (List procedures for strength reporting, replacements, casualty reporting, and other procedures pertinent to base defense.)

f. Civil Affairs. (Describe control of civil populations, refugees, and related matters.)

5.   Command and Signal

a. Communications. (Give information about pertinent communications nets, operating frequencies, codes and code words, recognition and identification procedures, and electronic emission constraints. Reference may be made to an annex or to a signal operating instruction.)

(1) Types

(a) Primary.

(b) Alternate.

(2) Operation.

(3) Maintenance.

(4) Authentication.

b. Command

(1) Joint and multinational relationships. (Command relationships must be spelled out clearly, to include command succession. Shifts in relationships as the defense progresses, as when a response force is committed, must be specified. These relationships may be presented in chart form as an annex.)

(2) Command posts and alternate command posts. (List locations of the BDOC, BCOC, and their alternate sites, along with the times of their activation and deactivation.)

6.   Acknowledgment Instructions

Annexes:
A. Task Organization
B. Intelligence
C. Operations
D. Logistics
E. Personnel
F. Public Affairs
G. Civil Affairs
H. Engineer Support
J. Command Relationships
K. Communications
L. Force Protection
M. Host-Nation Support
N. CBRN

Distribution:

Authentication:

APPENDIX C
REFERENCES

The development of Joint Pub 3-10 is based upon the following primary references.

1. **Department of Defense Publications**

    a. DODD 2000.12, *DOD Antiterrorism (AT) Program.*

    b. DODD O-2000.12-H, *DOD Antiterrorism Handbook.*

    c. DODD 3020.40, *Defense Critical Infrastructure Program (DCIP).*

    d. DODD 4500.54, *Official Temporary Duty Travel Abroad.*

    e. DODD 5105.75, *Department of Defense Operations at US Embassies.*

    f. DODI 1400.32, *DOD Civilian Work Force Contingency and Emergency Planning Guidelines and Procedures.*

    g. DODI 2000.16, *DOD Antiterrorism Standards.*

    h. DODI 3020.41, *Contractor Personnel Authorized to Accompany the US Armed Forces.*

    i. DODI 5210.84, *Security of DOD Personnel at US Missions Abroad.*

2. **Chairman of the Joint Chief of Staff Publications**

    a. Chairman of the Joint Chiefs of Staff Instruction (CJCSI) 3121.01B, *Standing Rules of Engagement.*

    b. CJCSI 5120.02A, *Joint Doctrine Development System.*

    c. CJCSI 5261.01A, *Combating Terrorism Readiness Initiatives Fund.*

    d. CJCSM 3113.01B, *Theater Security Cooperation.*

    e. CJCSM 3122.01A, *Joint Operation Planning and Execution System (JOPES) Volume I (Planning Policies and Procedures).*

    f. CJCSM 3122.02C, *Joint Operation Planning and Execution System (JOPES) Volume III (Crisis Action Time-Phased Force and Deployment Data Development and Deployment Execution).*

g. CJCSM 3122.03C, *Joint Operation Planning and Execution System Volume II, Planning Formats.*

h. CJCSM 3141.01A, *Procedures for the Review of Operation Plans.*

i. CJSCM 3500.05A, *Joint Task Force Headquarters Master Training Guide.*

3. **Joint Publications**

a. JP 1, *Doctrine for the Armed Forces of the United States.*

b. JP 2-0, *Joint Intelligence.*

c. JP 3-0, *Joint Operations.*

d. JP 3-01, *Countering Air and Missile Threats.*

e JP 3-02, *Amphibious Operations.*

f. JP 3-06, *Joint Urban Operations.*

g. JP 3-07.2, *Antiterrorism.*

h. JP 3-07.3, *Peace Operations.*

i. JP 3-08, *Interorganizational Coordination During Joint Operations.*

j. JP 3-09, *Joint Fire Support.*

k. JP 3-09.3, *Close Air Support.*

l. JP 3-11, *Operations in Chemical, Biological, Radiological, and Nuclear (CBRN) Environments.*

m. JP 3-13.3, *Operations Security.*

n. JP 3-13.4, *Military Deception.*

o. JP 3-15, *Barriers, Obstacles, and Mine Warfare for Joint Operations.*

p. JP 3-16, *Multinational Operations.*

q. JP 3-17, *Air Mobility Operations.*

r. JP 3-31, *Command and Control for Joint Land Forces.*

s. JP 3-34, *Joint Engineer Operations*.

t. JP 3-35, *Deployment and Redeployment Operations*.

u. JP 3-40, *Combating Weapons of Mass Destruction*.

v. JP 3-41, *Chemical, Biological, Radiological, and Nuclear Consequence Management*.

w. JP 3-63, *Detainee Operations*.

x. JP 4-0, *Joint Logistics*.

y. JP 4-02, *Health Service Support*.

z. JP 4-09, *Distribution Operations*.

aa. JP 4-10, *Operational Contract Support*.

bb. JP 6-0, *Joint Communications System*.

4. Multi-Service Publications

a. FM 3-07.31/MCWP 3-33.8/AFTTP(I) 3-2.40, *Multi-Service Tactics, Techniques, and Procedures for Conducting Peace Operations*.

b. FM 3-09.32/MCRP 3-16.6A/NTTP 3-09.2/AFTTP(I) 3-2.6, *Multi-Service Tactics, Techniques, and Procedures for the Joint Application of Firepower*.

c. FM 3-11.34/MCWP 3-37.5/NTTP 3-11.23/AFTTP(I) 3-2.33, *Multi-Service Tactics, Techniques, and Procedures for Installation Chemical, Biological, Radiological, and Nuclear Defense*.

d. FM 3-11.5/MCWP 3-37.3/NTTP 3-11.26/AFTTP (I) 3-2.60, *Multi-Service Tactics, Techniques, and Procedures for Installation Chemical, Biological, Radiological, and Nuclear Defense Decontamination*.

e. FM 3-55.6/MCRP 2-24A/NTTP 3-55.13/AFTTP(I) 3-2.2, *Multi-Service Tactics, Techniques, and Procedures for the Joint Surveillance Target Attack Radar System*.

f. FM 3-100.12/MCRP 5-12.1C/NTTP 5-03.5/AFTTP(I) 3-2.34, *Multi-Service Tactics, Techniques, and Procedures for Risk Management*.

g. FM 3-100.38/MCRP 3-17.2B/NTTP 3-02.41/AFTTP(I) 3-2.12, *Multi-Service Tactics, Techniques, and Procedures for Unexploded Ordnance (UXO) Operations*.

h. FM 4-01.45/MCRP 4-11.3H/NTTP 4-01.3/AFTTP 3-2.58, *Multi-Service Tactics, Techniques, and Procedures for Tactical Convoy Defense.*

5. **Army Publications**

a. Army Regulation 525-13, *Antiterrorism.*

b. FM 3-0, *Operations.*

c. FM 3-05.40, *Civil Affairs Operations.*

d. Army Tactics, Techniques, and Procedures (ATTP) 3-11.3, *Chemical, Biological, Radiological, and Nuclear Contamination Avoidance.*

e. ATTP 3-11.5, *Chemical, Biological, Radiological, and Nuclear Decontamination.*

f. FM 3-24, *Counterinsurgency Operations.*

g. FM 3-19.1, *Military Police Operations.*

h. ATTP 3-34.210, *Explosive Hazards Operations.*

i. ATTP 3-34.400, *General Engineering.*

j. FM 3-37, *Protection.*

k. FM 3-90, *Tactics.*

l. FM 3-90.31, *Maneuver Enhancement Brigade Operations.*

m. FM 3-100.21, *Contractors on the Battlefield.*

n. FM 4-01.30, *Army Movement Control.*

o. FM 4-93.4, *Theater Support Sustainment Command.*

p. TC 5-34, *Engineer Field Data.*

q. ATTP 22-6, *Guard Duty.*

r. ATTP 3-05.137, *Army Special Operating Forces Foreign Internal Defense, Tactics, Techniques, and Procedures for Special Forces.*

s. FM 2-01.3, *Intelligence Preparation of the Battlespace.*

t. FM 3-93, *Theater Army Headquarters.*

6. **Air Force Publications**

   a. AFDD 1, *Air Force Basic Doctrine*.

   b. AFDD 2, *Organization and Employment of Aerospace Power*.

   c. AFDD 2-4, *Combat Support*.

   d. AFDD 2-4.1, *Force Protection*.

   e. AFDD 2-4.4, *Bases, Infrastructure and Facilities*.

   f. AFDD 2-9, *Intelligence, Surveillance, and Reconnaissance Operations*.

   g. Air Force Policy Directive 31-3, *Air Base Defense*.

   h. Air Force Handbook (AFH) 10-222, *Guide on Bare Base Facility Erection*.

   i. AFH 31-302, *Air Base Defense Collective Skills*.

   j. AFH 31-305, *Security Forces Deployment Planning Handbook*.

   k. Air Force Instruction (AFI) 31-301, *Air Base Defense*.

   l. AFI 31-304(I), *Enemy Prisoners of War, Retained Personnel, Civilian Internees and Other Detainees*.

   m. AFTTP 3-10.1, *Integrated Base Defense*.

   n. AFTTP 3-10.2, *Integrated Base Defense Command and Control Tactics, Techniques, and Procedures*.

7. **Marine Corps Publications**

   a. Marine Corps Doctrine Publication (MCDP) 1-0, *Marine Corps Operations*.

   b. MCDP 4, *Logistics*.

   c. MCRP 3-15.2, *Mortars*.

   d. MCRP 3-41.1A, *MAGTF Rear Area Security*.

   e. MCRP 5-12D, *Organization of Marine Corps Forces*.

   f. MCWP 3-11.3, *Scouting and Patrolling*.

g. MCWP 3-16.6, *Supporting Arms Observer, Spotting, and Controller.*

h. MCWP 3-33.5, *Counterinsurgency Operations.*

i. MCWP 3-21.1, *Aviation Ground Support.*

j. MCWP 3-41.1, *Rear Area Operations.*

8. **Navy Publications**

a. NWP 3-10, *Naval Coastal Warfare.*

b. NWP 3-10.1, *Naval Coastal Warfare Operations.*

APPENDIX D
ADMINISTRATIVE INSTRUCTIONS

1. User Comments

Users in the field are highly encouraged to submit comments on this publication to: Commander, United States Joint Forces Command, Joint Warfighting Center, ATTN: Doctrine and Education Group, 116 Lake View Parkway, Suffolk, VA 23435-2697. These comments should address content (accuracy, usefulness, consistency, and organization), writing, and appearance.

2. Authorship

The lead agent for this publication is the US Army. The Joint Staff doctrine sponsor for this publication is the Director for Operations (J-3).

3. Supersession

This publication supersedes JP 3-10, 01 August 2006, *Joint Security Operations in Theater*.

4. Change Recommendations

a. Recommendations for urgent changes to this publication should be submitted:

```
TO:      CSA WASHINGTON DC//G-3/5//DAMO-SSP//
INFO:    JOINT STAFF WASHINGTON DC//J7-JEDD//
         CDRUSJFCOM SUFFOLK VA//JT10//
```

Routine changes should be submitted electronically to Commander, Joint Warfighting Center, Doctrine and Education Group and info the Lead Agent and the Director for Operational Plans and Joint Force Development J-7/JEDD via the CJCS JEL at http://www.dtic.mil/doctrine.

b. When a Joint Staff directorate submits a proposal to the Chairman of the Joint Chiefs of Staff that would change source document information reflected in this publication, that directorate will include a proposed change to this publication as an enclosure to its proposal. The Military Services and other organizations are requested to notify the Joint Staff J-7 when changes to source documents reflected in this publication are initiated.

c. Record of Changes:

CHANGE NUMBER	COPY NUMBER	DATE OF CHANGE	DATE ENTERED	POSTED BY	REMARKS

5. Distribution of Publications

Local reproduction is authorized and access to unclassified publications is unrestricted. However, access to and reproduction authorization for classified joint publications must be in accordance with DOD 5200.1-R, *Information Security Program*.

6. Distribution of Electronic Publications

a. Joint Staff J-7 will not print copies of JPs for distribution. Electronic versions are available on JDEIS at https://jdeis.js.mil (NIPRNET), and https://jdeis.js.smil.mil (SIPRNET) and on the JEL at http://www.dtic.mil/doctrine (NIPRNET).

b. Only approved joint publications and joint test publications are releasable outside the combatant commands, Services, and Joint Staff. Release of any classified joint publication to foreign governments or foreign nationals must be requested through the local embassy (Defense Attaché Office) to DIA Foreign Liaison Office, PO-FL, Room 1E811, 7400 Pentagon, Washington, DC 20301-7400.

c. CD-ROM. Upon request of a JDDC member, the Joint Staff J-7 will produce and deliver one CD-ROM with current joint publications.

GLOSSARY
PART I — ABBREVIATIONS AND ACRONYMS

AADC	area air defense commander
ADC	area damage control
AFDD	Air Force doctrine document
AFH	Air Force handbook
AFI	Air Force instruction
AFTTP	Air Force tactics, techniques, and procedures
AFTTP(I)	Air Force tactics, techniques, and procedures (instruction)
AMC	Air Mobility Command
AO	area of operations
AOR	area of responsibility
APOD	aerial port of debarkation
AT	antiterrorism
ATTP	Army tactics, techniques, and procedures
BCOC	base cluster operations center
BDOC	base defense operations center
C2	command and control
CAAF	contractors authorized to accompany the force
CAS	close air support
CBRN	chemical, biological, radiological, and nuclear
CCDR	combatant commander
CCIR	commander's critical information requirement
CI	counterintelligence
CISO	counterintelligence support officer
CJCSM	Chairman of the Joint Chiefs of Staff manual
CMO	civil-military operations
COM	chief of mission
COMMARFOR	commander, Marine Corps forces
DATT	defense attaché
DOD	Department of Defense
DODD	Department of Defense directive
DODI	Department of Defense instruction
EOD	explosive ordnance disposal
EPW	enemy prisoner of war
FC	fires cell (Army)
FM	field manual (Army)
FOB	forward operating base
FP	force protection

FPTAS	flight path threat analysis simulation
FPWG	force protection working group
FSCC	fire support coordination center
FSCM	fire support coordination measure
GCC	geographic combatant commander
HDC	harbor defense commander
HN	host nation
HNS	host-nation support
HUMINT	human intelligence
IADS	integrated air defense system
IAW	in accordance with
ICW	in coordination with
IED	improvised explosive device
IGO	intergovernmental organization
ISR	intelligence, surveillance, and reconnaissance
J-2	intelligence directorate of a joint staff
J-3	operations directorate of a joint staff
J-6	communications system directorate of a joint staff
JAOC	joint air operations center
JDDOC	joint deployment and distribution operations center
JFACC	joint force air component commander
JFC	joint force commander
JFLCC	joint force land component commander
JFMCC	joint force maritime component commander
JIOC	joint intelligence operations center
JIPOE	joint intelligence preparation of the operational environment
JISE	joint intelligence support element
JLSB	joint line of communications security board
JMC	joint movement center
JOA	joint operations area
JP	joint publication
JSA	joint security area
JSC	joint security coordinator
JSCC	joint security coordination center
JSO	joint security operations
JTF	joint task force
LOC	line of communications
MAGTF	Marine air-ground task force
MCDP	Marine Corps doctrine publication
MCM	mine countermeasures

MCRP	Marine Corps reference publication
MCWP	Marine Corps warfighting publication
MDSU	mobile diving and salvage unit
MESF	maritime expeditionary security force
METT-T	mission, enemy, terrain and weather, troops and support available — time available
MNF	multinational force
MOA	memorandum of agreement
MP	military police (Army and Marine)
MSF	mobile security force
MSR	main supply route
MSRON	maritime expeditionary security squadron
NAVELSG	Navy expeditionary logistics support group
NCO	noncommissioned officer
NGO	nongovernmental organization
NTTP	Navy tactics, techniques, and procedures
NWP	Navy warfare publication
OGA	other government agency
OP	observation post
OPCON	operational control
OPORD	operation order
OPSEC	operations security
PIR	priority intelligence requirement
PSU	port security unit
RAOC	rear area operations center
RIVRON	riverine squadron
ROE	rules of engagement
RSO	regional security officer
RTOC	rear tactical operations center
RUF	rules for the use of force
SAM	surface-to-air missile
SDO	senior defense official
SecDef	Secretary of Defense
SF	security forces (Air Force or Navy)
SITREP	situation report
SJA	staff judge advocate
SOFA	status-of-forces agreement
SPOD	seaport of debarkation
TACON	tactical control
TCF	tactical combat force

TCN	third country national
TIM	toxic industrial material
TSC	theater support command
UAS	unmanned aircraft system
UFC	Unified Facilities Criteria
USCG	United States Coast Guard
USG	United States Government
USTRANSCOM	United States Transportation Command
VAAP	vulnerability assessment and assistance program
VBIED	vehicle-borne improvised explosive device

Unless otherwise annotated, this publication is the proponent for all terms and definitions found in the glossary. Upon approval, JP 1-02, *Department of Defense Dictionary of Military and Associated Terms*, will reflect this publication as the source document for these terms and definitions.

alert force. Specified forces maintained in a special degree of readiness. (JP 1-02. SOURCE: JP 3-10)

area command. A command which is composed of those organized elements of one or more of the Armed Services, designated to operate in a specific geographical area, which are placed under a single commander. (JP 1-02. SOURCE: JP 3-10)

area damage control. Measures taken before, during, or after hostile action or natural or manmade disasters, to reduce the probability of damage and minimize its effects. Also called ADC. (JP 1-02. SOURCE: JP 3-10)

area of operations. An operational area defined by the joint force commander for land and maritime forces. Areas of operation do not typically encompass the entire operational area of the joint force commander, but should be large enough for component commanders to accomplish their missions and protect their forces. Also called AO. (JP 1-02. SOURCE: JP 3-0)

Army base. None. (Approved for removal from JP 1-02.)

axial route. None. (Approved for removal from JP 1-02.)

base. 1. A locality from which operations are projected or supported. 2. An area or locality containing installations which provide logistic or other support. 3. Home airfield or home carrier. (JP 1-02. SOURCE: JP 4-0)

base boundary. A line that delineates the surface area of a base for the purpose of facilitating coordination and deconfliction of operations between adjacent units, formations, or areas. (JP 1-02. SOURCE: 3-10)

base cluster. In base defense operations, a collection of bases, geographically grouped for mutual protection and ease of command and control. (JP 1-02. SOURCE: JP 3-10)

base cluster commander. In base defense operations, a senior base commander designated by the joint force commander responsible for coordinating the defense of bases within the base cluster and for integrating defense plans of bases into a base cluster defense plan. (JP 1-02. SOURCE: JP 3-10)

base cluster operations center. A command and control facility that serves as the base cluster commander's focal point for defense and security of the base cluster. Also called BCOC. (JP 1-02. SOURCE: JP 3-10)

base commander. In base defense operations, the officer assigned to command a base. (JP 1-02. SOURCE: JP 3-10)

base defense. The local military measures, both normal and emergency, required to nullify or reduce the effectiveness of enemy attacks on, or sabotage of, a base, to ensure that the maximum capacity of its facilities is available to US forces. (JP 1-02. SOURCE: JP 3-10)

base defense forces. Troops assigned or attached to a base for the primary purpose of base defense and security as well as augmentees and selectively armed personnel available to the base commander for base defense from units performing primary missions other than base defense. (JP 1-02. SOURCE: JP 3-10)

base defense operations center. A command and control facility, with responsibilities similar to a base cluster operations center, established by the base commander to serve as the focal point for base security and defense. It plans, directs, integrates, coordinates, and controls all base defense efforts. Also called BDOC. (JP 1-02. SOURCE: JP 3-10)

base defense zone. None. (Approved for removal from JP 1-02.)

chief of mission. The principal officer (the ambassador) in charge of a diplomatic facility of the United States, including any individual assigned to be temporarily in charge of such a facility. The chief of mission is the personal representative of the President to the country of accreditation. The chief of mission is responsible for the direction, coordination, and supervision of all US Government executive branch employees in that country (except those under the command of a US area military commander). The security of the diplomatic post is the chief of mission's direct responsibility. Also called COM. (JP 1-02. SOURCE: JP 3-08)

coastal sea control. The employment of forces to ensure the unimpeded use of an offshore coastal area by friendly forces and, as appropriate, to deny the use of the area to enemy forces. (JP 1-02. SOURCE: JP 3-10)

combat support elements. None. (Approved for removal from JP 1-02.)

combat support troops. None. (Approved for removal from JP 1-02.)

force protection. Preventive measures taken to mitigate hostile actions against Department of Defense personnel (to include family members), resources, facilities, and critical information. Force protection does not include actions to defeat the enemy or protect against accidents, weather, or disease. Also called FP. (JP 1-02. SOURCE: JP 3-0)

force protection working group. Cross-functional working group whose purpose is to conduct risk assessment and risk management and to recommend mitigating measures to the commander. Also called FPWG. (JP 1-02. SOURCE: JP 3-10)

harbor defense. None. (Approved for removal from JP 1-02.)

high-water mark. None. (Approved for removal from JP 1-02.)

joint base. For purposes of base defense operations, a joint base is a locality from which operations of two or more of the Military Departments are projected or supported and which is manned by significant elements of two or more Military Departments or in which significant elements of two or more Military Departments are located. (JP 1-02. SOURCE: JP 3-10)

joint line of communications security board. None. (Approved for removal from JP 1-02.)

joint security area. A specific surface area, designated by the joint force commander to facilitate protection of joint bases and their connecting lines of communications that support joint operations. Also called JSA. (This term and its definition modify the existing term and its definition and are approved for inclusion in JP 1-02.)

joint security coordination center. A joint operations center tailored to assist the joint security coordinator in meeting the security requirements in the joint operational area. Also called JSCC. (JP 1-02. SOURCE: JP 3-10)

joint security coordinator. The officer with responsibility for coordinating the overall security of the operational area in accordance with joint force commander directives and priorities. Also called JSC. (JP 1-02. SOURCE: JP 3-10)

mobile security force. A dedicated security force designed to defeat Level I and II threats on a base and/or base cluster. Also called MSF. (JP 1-02. SOURCE: JP 3-10)

movement control. 1. The planning, routing, scheduling, and control of personnel and cargo movements over lines of communications. 2. An organization responsible for the planning, routing, scheduling, and control of personnel and cargo movements over lines of communications. Also called movement control center or MCC. (JP 1-02. SOURCE: JP 3-10)

naval coastal warfare. None. (Approved for removal from JP 1-02.)

naval coastal warfare commander. None. (Approved for removal from JP 1-02.)

perimeter defense. None. (Approved for removal from JP 1-02.)

port security. The safeguarding of vessels, harbors, ports, waterfront facilities, and cargo from internal threats such as destruction, loss, or injury from sabotage or other subversive acts; accidents; thefts; or other causes of similar nature. (JP 1-02. SOURCE: JP 3-10)

rear area. None. (Approved for removal from JP 1-02.)

rear area operations center/rear tactical operations center. A command and control facility that serves as an area and/or subarea commander's planning, coordinating, monitoring, advising, and directing agency for area security operations. (JP 1-02. SOURCE: JP 3-10)

rear guard. None. (Approved for removal from JP 1-02.)

regional security officer. A security officer responsible to the chief of mission (ambassador), for security functions of all US embassies and consulates in a given country or group of adjacent countries. Also called RSO. (JP 1-02. SOURCE: JP 3-10)

response force. A mobile force with appropriate fire support designated, usually by the area commander to deal with Level II threats in the operational area. Also called RF. (This term and its definition modify the existing term and its definition and are approved for inclusion in JP 1-02.)

security. 1. Measures taken by a military unit, activity, or installation to protect itself against all acts designed to, or which may, impair its effectiveness. (JP 3-10) 2. A condition that results from the establishment and maintenance of protective measures that ensure a state of inviolability from hostile acts or influences. (JP 3-10) 3. With respect to classified matter, the condition that prevents unauthorized persons from having access to official information that is safeguarded in the interests of national security. (JP 2-0) (This term and its definition modify the existing term and its definition and are approved for inclusion in JP 1-02.)

sonic. None. (Approved for removal from JP 1-02.)

tactical combat force. A combat unit, with appropriate combat support and combat service support assets, that is assigned the mission of defeating Level III threats. Also called TCF. (JP 1-02. SOURCE: JP 3-10)

vehicle-borne improvised explosive device. A device placed or fabricated in an improvised manner on a vehicle incorporating destructive, lethal, noxious, pyrotechnic, or incendiary chemicals and designed to destroy, incapacitate, harass, or distract. Otherwise known as a car bomb. Also called VBIED. (JP 1-02. SOURCE: JP 3-10)

JOINT DOCTRINE PUBLICATIONS HIERARCHY

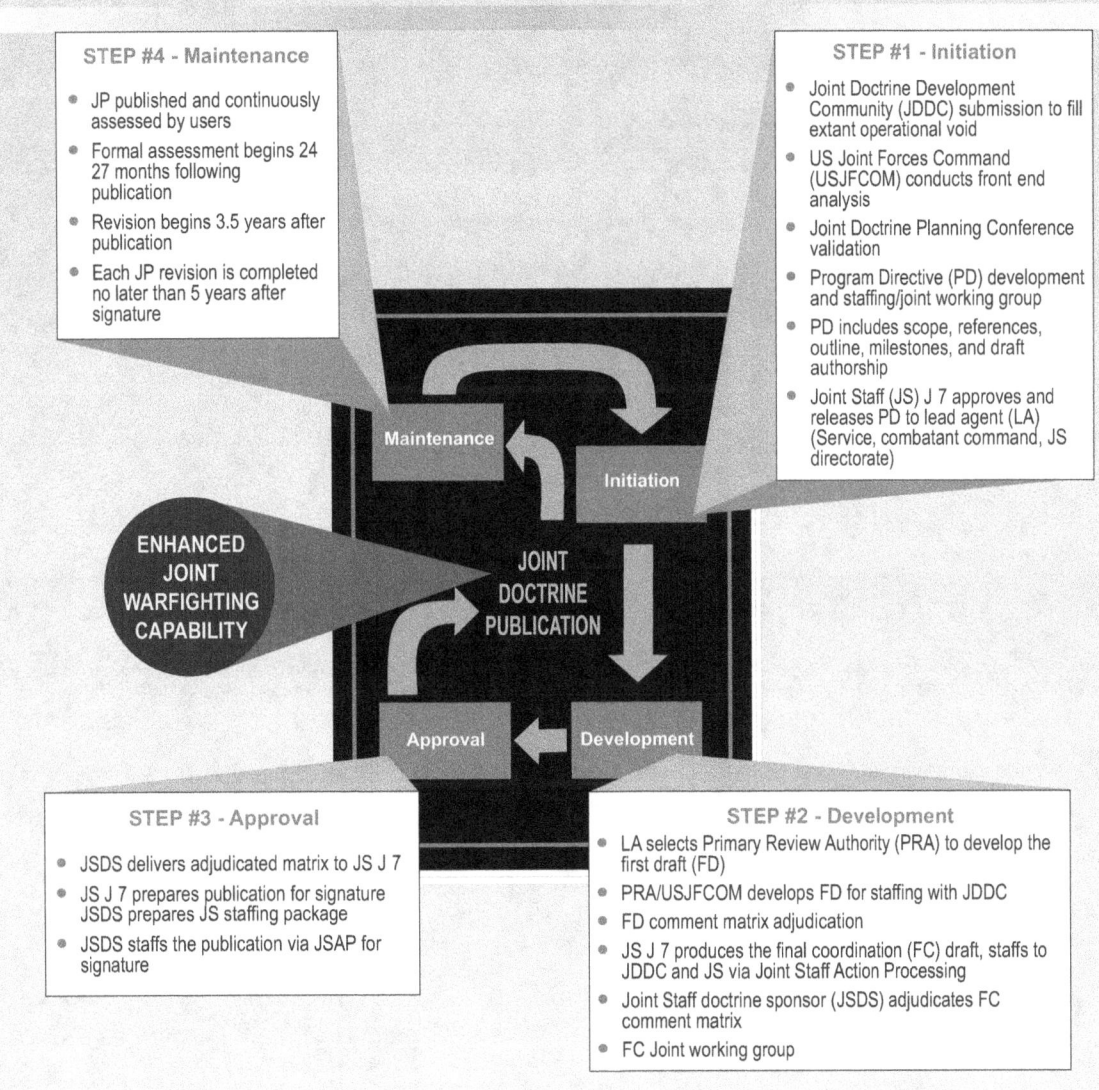

All joint publications are organized into a comprehensive hierarchy as shown in the chart above. **Joint Publication (JP) 3-10** is in the **Operations** series of joint doctrine publications. The diagram below illustrates an overview of the development process:

STEP #4 - Maintenance

- JP published and continuously assessed by users
- Formal assessment begins 24 27 months following publication
- Revision begins 3.5 years after publication
- Each JP revision is completed no later than 5 years after signature

STEP #1 - Initiation

- Joint Doctrine Development Community (JDDC) submission to fill extant operational void
- US Joint Forces Command (USJFCOM) conducts front end analysis
- Joint Doctrine Planning Conference validation
- Program Directive (PD) development and staffing/joint working group
- PD includes scope, references, outline, milestones, and draft authorship
- Joint Staff (JS) J 7 approves and releases PD to lead agent (LA) (Service, combatant command, JS directorate)

STEP #3 - Approval

- JSDS delivers adjudicated matrix to JS J 7
- JS J 7 prepares publication for signature JSDS prepares JS staffing package
- JSDS staffs the publication via JSAP for signature

STEP #2 - Development

- LA selects Primary Review Authority (PRA) to develop the first draft (FD)
- PRA/USJFCOM develops FD for staffing with JDDC
- FD comment matrix adjudication
- JS J 7 produces the final coordination (FC) draft, staffs to JDDC and JS via Joint Staff Action Processing
- Joint Staff doctrine sponsor (JSDS) adjudicates FC comment matrix
- FC Joint working group

www.ingramcontent.com/pod-product-compliance
Lightning Source LLC
Chambersburg PA
CBHW081326310526
45789CB00018B/2412